D0596773

Property of
Baker College of
Allen Park

365

Low or No Cost Workplace

Teambuilding Activities

Games and Exercises Designed to Build Trust and Encourage Teamwork Among Employees

By John Peragine, Jr.

365 LOW OR NO COST WORKPLACE TEAMBUILDING ACTIVITIES: GAMES AND EXERCISES DESIGNED TO BUILD TRUST AND ENCOURAGE TEAMWORK AMONG EMPLOYEES

Copyright © 2007 by Atlantic Publishing Group, Inc.
1405 SW 6th Ave. • Ocala, Florida 34471 • 800-814-1132 • 352-622-1875–Fax
Web site: www.atlantic-pub.com • E-mail: sales@atlantic-pub.com
SAN Number: 268-1250

No part of this publication may be reproduced, stored in a retrieval system, or transmitted in any form or by any means, electronic, mechanical, photocopying, recording, scanning, or otherwise, except as permitted under Section 107 or 108 of the 1976 United States Copyright Act, without the prior written permission of the Publisher. Requests to the Publisher for permission should be sent to Atlantic Publishing Group, Inc., 1405 SW 6th Ave., Ocala, Florida 34471.

ISBN-13: 978-1-60138-043-2   ISBN-10: 1-60138-043-7

Library of Congress Cataloging-in-Publication Data

Peragine, John N., 1970-
  365 low or no cost workplace teambuilding activities : games and exercises designed to build trust and encourage teamwork among employees / by John N. Peragine.
      p. cm.
  Includes bibliographical references and index.
  ISBN-13: 978-1-60138-043-2 (alk. paper)
  ISBN-10: 1-60138-043-7 (alk. paper)
  1. Teams in the workplace. 2. Interpersonal communication. 3. Communication in organizations. I. Title. II. Title: Three hundred sixty five low or no cost workplace teambuilding activities.

  HD66.P427 2008
  658.4'022--dc22
                    2007049119

LIMIT OF LIABILITY/DISCLAIMER OF WARRANTY: The publisher and the author make no representations or warranties with respect to the accuracy or completeness of the contents of this work and specifically disclaim all warranties, including without limitation warranties of fitness for a particular purpose. No warranty may be created or extended by sales or promotional materials. The advice and strategies contained herein may not be suitable for every situation. This work is sold with the understanding that the publisher is not engaged in rendering legal, accounting, or other professional services. If professional assistance is required, the services of a competent professional should be sought. Neither the publisher nor the author shall be liable for damages arising herefrom. The fact that an organization or Web site is referred to in this work as a citation and/or a potential source of further information does not mean that the author or the publisher endorses the information the organization or Web site may provide or recommendations it may make. Further, readers should be aware that Internet Web sites listed in this work may have changed or disappeared between when this work was written and when it is read.

Printed on Recycled Paper

INTERIOR LAYOUT DESIGN: Vickie Taylor • vtaylor@atlantic-pub.com

Printed in the United States

We recently lost our beloved pet "Bear," who was not only our best and dearest friend but also the "Vice President of Sunshine" here at Atlantic Publishing. He did not receive a salary but worked tirelessly 24 hours a day to please his parents. Bear was a rescue dog that turned around and showered myself, my wife Sherri, his grandparents Jean, Bob and Nancy and every person and animal he met (maybe not rabbits) with friendship and love. He made a lot of people smile every day.

We wanted you to know that a portion of the profits of this book will be donated to The Humane Society of the United States.

–Douglas & Sherri Brown

THE HUMANE SOCIETY
OF THE UNITED STATES ©

The human-animal bond is as old as human history. We cherish our animal companions for their unconditional affection and acceptance. We feel a thrill when we glimpse wild creatures in their natural habitat or in our own backyard.

Unfortunately, the human-animal bond has at times been weakened. Humans have exploited some animal species to the point of extinction.

The Humane Society of the United States makes a difference in the lives of animals here at home and worldwide. The HSUS is dedicated to creating a world where our relationship with animals is guided by compassion. We seek a truly humane society in which animals are respected for their intrinsic value, and where the human-animal bond is strong.

Want to help animals? We have plenty of suggestions. Adopt a pet from a local shelter, join The Humane Society and be a part of our work to help companion animals and wildlife. You will be funding our educational, legislative, investigative and outreach projects in the U.S. and across the globe.

Or perhaps you'd like to make a memorial donation in honor of a pet, friend or relative? You can through our Kindred Spirits program. And if you'd like to contribute in a more structured way, our Planned Giving Office has suggestions about estate planning, annuities, and even gifts of stock that avoid capital gains taxes.

Maybe you have land that you would like to preserve as a lasting habitat for wildlife. Our Wildlife Land Trust can help you. Perhaps the land you want to share is a backyard—that's enough. Our Urban Wildlife Sanctuary Program will show you how to create a habitat for your wild neighbors.

So you see, it's easy to help animals. And The HSUS is here to help.

The Humane Society of the United States
2100 L Street NW
Washington, DC 20037
202-452-1100
www.hsus.org

Author Dedication & Biography

I dedicate this book to my loving wife, Kate, and my patient children, Sarah and Loreena. A special thanks to my mentor Pete Ballard who taught me all there is to know about a preposition.

John N. Peragine

John N. Peragine, PhD, is a freelance writer and classical musician. He has been in the human services field for more than thirteen years. John holds a B.S. in psychology from Appalachian State University. When John is not writing, he plays the piccolo in the Western Piedmont Symphony.

Table of Contents

Preface

When it comes to manpower, a team can equal much more than the sum of its parts. The operative word here is can. There are certainly instances in which the opposite is true. A team can work with the finesse of a symphony, playing perfect harmonies. The music they create can bring you to tears over the beauty and absolute perfection of the teamwork being conducted by their leader, the maestro.

In contrast, a team that is not working together is like a horrible train wreck. Instead of creating beautiful music, they create a cacophony that would make a dog howl. This book is created with the goal of taking a group of strangers and getting them to work in harmony with reduced conflict and miscommunication that often plague teams.

The leader of a team sets the beat that the rest of the team follows. Effective teamwork requires effective leadership, so the place to start in building a team is putting a leader in charge who does not exhibit destructive characteristics. Are good leaders hard to find? Of course they are, but taking the time to identify and make an investment in strong leaders is money in the bank. It is much easier to start with a diamond than try to make one out of coal. Some great leaders may be diamonds in the rough, but they are still diamonds.

In 1968, Dr. Lawrence J. Peter wrote a book called the *Peter Principle*, which outlines the tendency of large corporations, including governmental agencies, to promote people who are not necessarily cut out for the position. He claims that, "In a hierarchy every employee tends to rise to his level of incompetence." Although an employee may have excellent skills as a worker, he may not have the necessary skills to become a manager. So what are the hallmarks of effective leadership?

- Building loyalty

- Modeling effective behavior

- Inspiring employees

- Achieving buy-in

- Weeding out the uncommitted

- Holding the team together over the long term

- Managing time effectively

- Avoiding "hoarding" of knowledge

- Working across employee levels

- Producing results

Once a good leader is chosen, this book will be an invaluable tool. A leader can rally his troops to do many extraordinary things. This book gives a manager the tools and exercises necessary to conduct a beautiful symphony.

You will notice that analogies of a conductor and symphony are offered frequently as analogies for a leader and team. I picked these analogies for a couple of reasons. The first is because I am a musician. I have played with orchestras for many years and know how they work and what makes a great orchestra as opposed to a mediocre one.

The other reason is that an orchestra is the perfect example of a leader and team working together. You can actually hear the teamwork happening and you can definitely hear when it is not. This analogy can work for any team or organization. The premise is the same — the leader leads and gets a team to accomplish a goal. It does not matter whether it is to play a concerto, create furniture in a factory, respond to a tragedy in New Orleans after a hurricane, or provide coffee at a local church every Sunday. The principles are the same for a successful team. What makes this book so invaluable is its flexibility in many different environments and situations.

Note: In much of this book, I use the pronoun "he." This does not suggest that women are not effective leaders. It is meant to be only a convenient placeholder for ease of reading and consistency.

Teambuilding activities are designed to help a group of people trust and communicate more effectively, in order to facilitate a more productive work or organizational environment.

Stephen Coenen

Teambuilding activities are any strategies that a group leader employs to get members of the group to work together in becoming more productive and happier in their jobs. In the theatre, there are many types of exercises used to accomplish this. Warm-up activities and improvisations are most commonly used.

Teambuilding exercises are beneficial because they help each person understand how everyone else on the team works. Participation in teambuilding exercises gives people a common ground of experience they can talk about later. Particularly for those in the entertainment business, teambuilding exercises are important because the business is so stressful and demanding. Taking a little time from the tasks at hand in order to bond with colleagues will help the tasks go faster when the team gets back to their to-do lists.

Kim Stinson

There are two types of teambuilding:

- Building a team for a project/initiative

- Building a team for an ongoing growth of the company

Teambuilding Activity Definition: Teambuilding activities are a series of actions you take to bring a group together so that they can work in a cohesive manner. The activities must include auditory, visual, and kinesthetic so that they have a lasting impact. They could be fun exercises to break the ice, informational and educational to bring everyone on the same page, or kinesthetic for people to experience a simulated environment which could reflect reality.

Companies and organizations should use teambuilding exercises to:

- Solve a problem

- Create focus/bring the team on the same page

- Focus on common issues facing the team versus personal issues

- Learn as a team and from each other

- Resolve personal/departmental conflicts and establish better understanding of different personalities

Pramod Goel

Introduction

Roadmap to Success — Teamwork

To begin, let us have a working definition of what a team is. Team is a word like "family" that has many meanings and everyone may have a different idea of what a team should be.

There are many different kinds of teams. Below is a list of a few common types and their descriptions.

Project Teams

These are specific teams created to complete a project. They are usually temporary, only exist while the project is being completed, and are disbanded after the project is completed. A committee created to search for the director of a hospital is an example. The members are from different disciplines in the hospital and have input from their individual departments. Once a director is hired, the committee no longer exists. Even though these teams are temporary, they still can benefit from teambuilding activities. These are usually people who have not worked together before. Rapport building and cooperative play exercises can assist these types of teams to accomplish their goal faster and more efficiently. The group learns to work together without the pressure of a deadline. Teambuilding activities at the beginning and throughout the team's existence can help keep things fresh and moving. Some of the exercises can help get a stuck team unstuck. The exercises help the team be creative and problem solve as a group rather than as a collection of individuals.

Every time a new person comes into a class I do teambuilding activities. Everyone starts at a baseline in the group, no matter what their background is. This allows people already in the class to welcome that new person and help them along.

Sonya Briggs

Working Teams

These are teams that work together everyday with a purpose. The group is more permanent than the project team, although team members may come and go. Their purpose can be flexible. Here are some subcategories of working teams:

- An obvious work team: This type of team forms because a group of individuals are working together in a specific area, like a nursing staff.

- An obvious team with a purpose: This is a group of individuals that must accomplish common tasks together. In a nursing situation, this may be the group of nurses responsible for the intensive care unit.

- Management team: This team is responsible for managing and directing a group of specific individuals. They coordinate activities, monitor their individual teams, and collaborate to encourage their teams to work together. When I worked for social service agencies there was a supervisor over each unit — welfare, child welfare, food stamps, adult welfare, and Medicaid. These supervisors, under the leadership of the agency director, made up the management team. They talked about issues that affected more than one unit.

All teams benefit tremendously from the exercises outlined in this book. There are exercises that help these teams interact with each other for the first time, exercises that help them communicate better with one another, and exercises that help develop self-esteem within the team. A number of professionals helped develop this book and all agree that teambuilding exercises should occur on a regular basis, especially when members of the team leave or are added.

Virtual Teams

In the world of technology, there is a new breed of team — the virtual team. People now work together over great distances without actually meeting in person. These virtual teams can encounter a number of communication problems. The Internet and e-mail are not always the best medium to communicate clearly. Talking on the phone is a little better, but you still cannot see a person's body language or other nonverbal communications.

It is not always possible to get virtual teams together physically. Conference calls and online chats are recommended on a regular basis to make sure everyone is working together and communicating. Some of these exercises can be altered to work in the virtual world. If at all possible, a person-to-person meeting can do wonders for a virtual team.

To summarize, a team is defined as a group of individuals who work together. This may seem simple and a little vague, but this definition allows for any kind of group to be considered a team. Whether it be members of a baseball team, Girl Scout troupe, NASCAR pit crew, or a Fortune 500 corporation, they all have commonalities such as shared purpose, the need for open communication, and the need for strong leadership.

Winning Team Leaders

The search is on for a conductor of the Chicago Symphony. A committee has been formed in order to find the right conductor to lead the orchestra. What characteristics should the committee be looking for? How can they be sure that the person who is chosen will develop an orchestra that will meet the standards of a world class symphony in which patrons buy season tickets year after year? A team is only as good as its leader. It is essential that the person hired for the position not be promoted based upon the Peter Principle but rather on essential qualities of a successful leader.

I may be stern with my students, but I am the role model for behavior in the studio and especially when they go out on stage to perform. I allow them to have fun; at the same time they learn to be disciplined and work together. Everyone relies on everyone else when it comes to a team.

Sonya Briggs

Role Model

A leader must be a dynamic and powerful role model, a person the team wants to emulate. Ideally, this person will not only be well-qualified but also have significant experience. In our example, the Chicago Symphony has a high standard and wants to choose a person that has experience conducting other symphonies. The leader should have a strong reputation, strong ethics, and inspire those under his management. It is difficult for a leader to ask his people to accomplish things that he is not able or willing to do himself.

Initiative and Entrepreneurial Drive

A leader must be creative in leading the team in new directions. For example, a conductor selects the music, chooses new venues for performance, and works with the orchestra board in coming up with fundraising activities. Teams need leaders who not only establish ambitious and worthwhile goals, but also aggressively pursue them with the assistance of a well-coordinated team.

Personality

Ambitious planning and execution, while essential qualities, does not get a team very far if others are unwilling to cooperate with the leader.

Many people with excellent leadership skills fail because they are unable to achieve buy-in. If individuals are committed to the goals laid down by their leader, the goals are much easier to achieve. If they are not, very little will be accomplished. The leader must be likeable, personable, a good listener, compassionate in his dealings with his people, and flexible enough that everyone is comfortable with his leadership. If the team members genuinely like and admire him, they will follow him anywhere. In dealing with territorial issues, jealousy, or competitiveness, a winsome personality goes a long way toward solving serious conflicts. If a leader is hired from within and has a negative relationship with his peers or a history of not following the directions given to him by his superiors, he will not likely improve if he is promoted.

Commitment

The effective leader is one who believes he can make a difference and is so committed to the cause that it tends to take over his life, professional and private. He must believe in the value of what that team does and be unfailingly committed to its mission and goals. Otherwise, he will not be able to inspire the members of his team, from the least to the most important, to catch the fire of commitment. He should believe that the group can make a difference. His passion should be especially evident in the type of language and attitude he shows on a daily basis.

Cooperation

Some people are, by their nature, obstinate when it comes to getting along with others. This is not a characteristic that leads to effective leadership. A good question to ask in choosing a leader is whether he exhibits a cooperative spirit. Is he willing to listen to others' opinions and ideas and, at times, replace his own with new or better approaches? Everyone has a voice and people make stronger team members if they are able to contribute more than just their time and effort.

Optimism

The effective leader keeps his team members' spirits up even in the event of disappointment. The leader must believe that established goals are going to be achieved and that any roadblock can be overcome. If he does not believe this, the members of his team will not either. A leader sets the tone and atmosphere for his team. If he is negative, his team will follow suit. If, on the other hand, he is positive, smiles, and talks about how much the team is accomplishing and identifies individuals' successes, the team will be positive and motivated to work harder.

Self-Knowledge

Nothing puts a damper on a team more than a leader who has illusions about who he is — his self-worth and his persona. A leader should work these matters out long before he decides to assume the role of leader. Only with secure and accurate self-knowledge is the leader able to establish authenticity, which is important in leading others. A leader who is not honest in self-evaluation tends either to be too tentative or too overbearing to inspire the confidence and trust of those who are working with and under him. There is a delicate balance between the two, and a good leader knows when and when not to act.

Self-Awareness

While this may seem the same as self-knowledge, it is worthwhile to look at the two characteristics separately. Even a person who is secure in who he is and is not preoccupied with defining himself may not be able to use that knowledge to achieve a level of self-awareness that makes it possible for him to function effectively as the leader of a team. For example, he may overlook how others view him. He may feel that he can show up late because he is, after all, in charge; but such behavior will cost him dearly in the commitment of his team members. The leader should at all times be aware of his role and his influence with his members. Even if he has a sense of commitment to the team and to the objectives, if that is not clear to his team, he will not be successful. The leader must have a self-awareness of his strengths and faults. He is not afraid to make a mistake, but he acknowledges his mistakes and takes responsibility for his actions.

Ability to Choose Successful Team Members

A conductor may not be able to choose the members of his orchestra. The individuals may be selected by an orchestra committee. Even so, the conductor can designate roles in such a way that each member will be productive. He can quickly determine which ones are self-starters and do not need a lot of encouragement or prodding to stay on the job. He can also identify those with leadership potential who can lead their own teams to success.

Listening

The last characteristic that a leader should have is the ability and willingness to listen. It seems a minor thing, but it is not. So many talented, effective people are not as successful as they could be because they need to develop this skill. Listening is not waiting until the other person is finished talking so you can take the floor. Listening is more than hearing – it is caring about what the other person has to say and using leading questions. A good listener does not pretend to care; he actually does. A good leader will have that kind of concern and interest in other people. There are two terms that you will see throughout this book: active listening and empathic listening.

Active listening is the technique of really listening to the person talking to you. Remember that you cannot talk and listen at the same time. Listen, reframe, and repeat. Stephen R. Covey states in his book, *The Seven Habits of Highly Effective People*, that, when trying to communicate with another person, you should first attempt to understand then to be understood. This is the foundation of active listening. When you reframe what you hear, you are able to repeat back to the person what they just said. This is not parroting back exactly what he says, but rephrasing what you hear. This implores the other person to either agree or disagree with your interpretation of his point. This does two things: First, it increases solid communication and understanding, and second, it makes the person feel like he is being heard and that you are paying attention to him.

Empathic listening can be used at the same time as active listening. This goes beyond the concept of listening and reframing what is said to you. It includes body language, the removal of distractions, strong eye contact, and small responses that indicate that you understand and agree with what the speaker is saying and that what he is saying matters. This can be as simple as a head nod or a statement like, "Go on, I'm listening." This promotes trust, a deeper level of communication, and the message that you care what he has to say. That does not mean that you agree with the content of what he says, rather that you are really listening and understand his point of view.

Selecting a leader with these qualities is the most important factor in building an effective team. Even if all other qualities are present in the team itself, without a successful leader, goals will not be realized.

In order for a company to really benefit from teambuilding, there has got to be buy-in by middle management and front line managers. In order for there to be a real change in a team, it begins with the leaders and has a trickle down effect.

Dan Come

The Hallmarks of Effective Leadership

Building Loyalty

The Japanese-American soldiers in the 100th Infantry Battalion in World

War II were loyal to their leader, Young Oak Kim, a Korean, in spite of the soldiers' lifelong orientation that rejected everything Korean. Kim achieved this kind of loyalty because of his remarkable leadership abilities. He was a role model for his men — putting himself in danger before expecting them to do so. He was committed to the goal of overcoming the evil that had been introduced into the world by Adolph Hitler and believed that he and his men could make a difference. He had remarkable self-knowledge that made it possible for him to look beyond past injustices and willingly commit to the leadership of the Japanese-American battalion. The soldiers were willing to follow Kim wherever he led them.

Inspiring Employees

It is one thing for a leader to be inspired to commit to a cause and to work to achieve results, but if he is unable to communicate that to his followers, his commitment is of little effect. If the members of the team consider that what they are engaged in is just another day or week or month at work, little will be accomplished. It is the mark of an effective leader that members of the team buy-in to his commitment.

It is amazing to me that organizations will tolerate poor quality supervisors who are negative about their jobs and create dissension and mistrust on their teams. An organization must have the discipline and managerial courage to deal with those who are not supporting the organization's goals and a teamwork environment, either through training, improvement plans, reassignment to nonsupervisory jobs, or dismissal as a last resort.

Stephen Coenen

Weeding Out the Uncommitted

Uncommitted members must be weeded out because they will undermine the work of the team and erode the spirit that leads to success. This is not easy to do; there is always the concern that eliminating a member may lead to the same result — a diminishing of enthusiasm. It can create fear and mistrust, as other members of the team may feel that they are next in line to be fired. It takes a high level of leadership skill to achieve the whittling of the team without destroying the morale of the other team members. Communication and the opportunity for the remaining members of the team to discuss their feelings and fears are paramount. Reinforcement of the trust and cohesiveness of the team is imperative and should be a priority for the leader.

Holding the Team Together Over the Long Term

It is difficult to sustain commitment to projects that run for a fairly long period of time without any realization of achievement or success. An effective leader is aware of this hazard and continuously works to keep his team members involved. One way to do this is by meeting regularly and using the time together as a spirit-builder. Reminding the team of how far they have come is helpful in keeping the group involved. Rewarding team members in a tangible way for their roles in moving the project ahead is helpful. Many of the games and activities included in this book are useful for these purposes.

Breaking down large projects into smaller pieces can help keep interest in a project. Rewarding team members when each of these smaller segments is completed can be more effective than waiting until the end. For instance, let us suppose you have a large quota of sofas that need to be produced at the end of the month. If the quota is reached, a large bonus is awarded. Consider breaking down the monthly quota to individual quotas at the end of each week. Offer a small bonus each week for making the weekly quota. This gives a more immediate reward for the desired goal of the team. Also, if the team does not have a particularly good week, they can make it up the following week. This keeps morale and interest up while still achieving the long-term goal.

Companies without an identifiable desired outcome shouldn't use teambuilding exercises. Teambuilding and training programs have taken criticism as "feel good" activities and have been labeled expensive and expendable due to unclear and undefined goals.

A company should utilize teambuilding as part of a well defined messaging program that adds value to the individual's role, is process-driven to allow the individuals within a team to understand their role, and goal-oriented so the individual value is realized when the team is successful.

Companies should use teambuilding as a memorable and unique tool to deliver key beliefs and standards regarding communication, expectations, role identity, task sequencing, benchmarking, task management, and the benefit of assisting others in being successful.

Breon Klopp

Managing Time Effectively

Many teams fail in spite of best intentions and great commitment because time drifts away like sand through the fingers. A good leader manages this part of the project effectively. He establishes and enforces timelines. If a part of the team is falling behind, he takes action immediately to see that the members get back on track. Letting it continue can be destructive. Other team members will lose enthusiasm and overall commitment will slip.

Time management does not mean micro management. Employees usually do not enjoy someone over their shoulder every day, checking every little thing they do. It is not the best way to manage time, as it is distracting and stops the flow of work. Breaking down big projects into more manageable pieces is a proven approach to time management. Once you have established what each team member needs to complete their task, check in with them periodically. Having a set time to review what has been done and what the next step is makes the work flow easier, while still holding the team accountable.

In a symphony, a conductor has a certain amount of time to get a performance ready. This time is broken up over a preset number of rehearsals and the rehearsals have a set time. A conductor must decide how to use this time in the most efficient way with the goal of a flawless performance. The conductor is constantly reevaluating what he needs to do with the time he has been allotted. He must decide during a rehearsal what passages need to be worked on and how much time to allot to each piece of music that is going to be performed at a particular concert. This is reevaluated between rehearsals as the conductor prepares the schedule based on how well the previous session went. If the conductor squanders time, the performance will be negatively affected. Even worse, the musicians will question the skills and effectiveness of the conductor as a leader.

Teamwork is essential if the skills of the musicians are to be used successfully to ensure the best quality music. The same is true of other businesses as well. The chapters of this book will provide suggestions, tools, and approaches that will equip the leader to manage a well-coordinated and productive workforce.

A company should begin their teambuilding work with management, especially front line supervisors. That way the supervisors are ready to implement what the employees will learn from teambuilding activities. They can also encourage the employees under them that it is important and that they believe that changes are possible with everyone working together.

Dan Comer

1 What Are Teambuilding Activities & Why Should Your Company Be Using Them?

I personally believe the term "teambuilding" is misapplied to a large number of activities that are really a "shared experience," which are actually competitive in nature or may simply create a commonality among the participants to generate interaction (go-cart racing). These types of activities are certainly useful but do little to ultimately build the characteristics of a functioning team.

Additionally, most persons would define teambuilding as bringing a group together while consciously downplaying the role of individual performance. However, every organization functions in a manner based on individual success and no team is successful without the success of each piece of that team.

Teambuilding is activities structured in a manner that allows individuals to identify and maximize their competencies and perform tasks in a manner that contributes toward clear goals and the success of the entire team. In turn, the success of the team is based on the performance and action of each individual.

In pit crew teambuilding the team goal, as in real race competition, is to perform a series of tasks (new tires, fuel, adjustments, and reset) with quality and velocity (accuracy and speed). While the team accomplishes the pit stop, each individual is responsible for completing very specific tasks that allow the other team members to complete their specific tasks. When a single team member fails to complete their designated task with optimal performance, the entire team objective (time) is affected.

Breon Klopp

Forming teams to accomplish goals is as old as humanity itself. Even in primitive times, when a village or a culture was threatened, the inhabitants became a team, sometimes called an army, to defend their homes or livelihoods. Games involving teams can be found in ancient history. Either there is an innate tendency to band together with others with like interests to accomplish goals or man's reasoning capability determines that a team equals more than the sum of its parts. However, even animals grasp this way of getting the work done. A band of wolves with a common goal, for example, can do much more harm than a single one.

Teams and teamwork have become fields of study of their own, attracting professionals who become experts in the subject. They become consultants, trainers, and writers, advising companies and organizations on how to use teams to meet the challenges of a volatile business environment, no matter what area of the economy.

Not everyone is on the team bandwagon. Some see it as just a fad that will pass and that, in the long run, it is not particularly useful in managing business. Detractors point out that using this organizational model takes longer and leads to time-wasting. They see team meetings, especially those in which team games are used to improve how everyone works together, as a costly waste of time. However, many businesses that have come to the forefront in their own areas, such as Motorola, credit a shift from traditional organizational structures and management approaches to one that is based on teams and teamwork for their turnarounds from mediocrity to excellence.

This chapter will discuss the various roles that make up a successful team and how those roles work together to improve outcomes.

The Leader (Conductor)

The leader is sometimes referred to as the supervisor or coordinator. In the Preface and Introduction, we defined the team leader in terms of ideal characteristics. This chapter will carry that definition further and recommend functions for this role. I will use the example of a symphony throughout this and succeeding chapters. The reason this works as such a powerful metaphor is the image and function of a symphony. The conductor stands in front of his team and each member looks to the conductor for direction. Now, the conductor does not actually make the music; that is the role of the musicians. Each player is an expert in their instrument and knows how to perform his chosen part. Without the conductor, music could not be performed. No one would know when to start or stop, slow down or speed up, when to get soft or loud. The conductor is literally up before the symphony on a box so that everyone can see him. He is the defined team leader and keeps the music flowing. Following are some typical functions for the team leader:

- First and foremost makes certain that the work gets done and that objectives are actively pursued.

- Troubleshoots conflicts and breakdowns.

- Is cheerleader and encourager.

- Tends to team spirit. When morale fluctuates, the leader steps in to get things going again.

- Puts in place a data-based process that will provide the foundation for eventual success.

- Is communication central, not only for members of the team but also for others who will need to know about the activities and schedules for the team.

- Maintains records of meetings and decisions that were made.

- Leads discussions effectively so that even timid or tentative members feel free to express themselves and participate.

- Is a hands-on participant. He makes sure jobs are covered when a team member needs help.

- Has authority to implement changes. In instances that go beyond his or her authority, the leader takes requests to appropriate authority.

This list usually only touches on the many things the leader of a successful team will do, and the duties, activities, etc. of this position fluctuates according to the purpose and makeup of the team. However, an effective leader develops and sharpens skills for assigning roles, taking into account the background, preparation, personality, and experience of each member. This task should be taken very seriously and the leader should devote the time necessary to make good choices. Mistakes are always made in these choices, and a good leader will acknowledge them and take quick action to shift roles to the best advantage.

A team member may not be satisfied with the role he or she is given. For example, there may be too much or too little work or the person may have a very low level of interest in a particular function. It is important to be ready and willing to make adjustments, even to shift roles. Also, members must be willing to move outside their own roles from time to time and help others. That is what teamwork is all about.

Team Members (The Musicians)

Some members of a team may be passive in their roles, which is certain to defeat the efforts of the team and prevent the achievement of goals. Members need to understand that they are selected to serve on the team, not occupy a chair. If the leader is effective at communicating the mission and in fostering team spirit, this should not happen. Many of the games in Chapter 5 are useful for developing commitment and buy-in if they are used as intended. Following are characteristics of an effective team member:

Property of
Baker College of
Allen Park

- Assumes ownership of his or her role. Is a self-starter and does not need continual urging by the leader to get the work done.

- Willingly assists the leader at all times, even in the nuts and bolts of running a meeting, such as setting up audiovisual equipment, etc.

- Is not timid about entering into discussions and is willing to risk having opinions challenged.

- Always comes to meetings prepared and is cooperative in the leader's efforts to use meeting time judiciously and effectively.

- Does not take up meeting time with personal anecdotes or conversation.

- Is a good listener, open to the ideas of others, and willing to change his or her mind.

- Does not dominate discussions.

- Is able and willing to prepare reports and make presentations.

- Diligently and conscientiously carries out assignments and responsibilities. Comes to each meeting prepared to report progress.

- Is willing to go outside his or her own area of responsibility to help another team member. On the other hand, the member does not slack off and then expect others to do his or her job.

In a symphony, a musician must be prepared for each rehearsal (meeting). He has to have his music, his music stand, and his instrument. He must take total responsibility for being prepared. There is no excuse for not having music on the stand ready to play when the conductor raises his baton. If a musician's instrument needs repair or a new reed, he does not expect the conductor to provide this for him. A musician has to take care of his own needs. If another musician needs help, like a pencil to mark the music, he is always willing to lend a hand. It is the team that matters, not the individual. If one musician is not prepared, it can throw off the rest of the musicians.

A symphony plays as an ensemble. When you listen to a piece of music, you hear it as a whole — each instrument playing in harmony with every other instrument. No one player is sticking out by trying to play over the others. There are times in music when the solo or particular section is called out to play over the symphony, but this is planned and conducted.

In the business world teams assign roles, such as recorder, time keeper, facilitator, advisor, or process coach when they are having weekly meetings. All these are important functional roles for the team, and most team members know their job-related roles. A team should also consider the natural roles people bring to the team. Each team member brings his own strengths. Some are good organizers, some are creative, and some are good conflict managers. The team should be aware of these natural attributes and use them to contribute to the effort. This helps to include everyone in the process while allowing people to shine.

Communication

If the team is the vehicle, then communication is the key to unlock and drive that vehicle. In Chapter 4 you will find exercises specifically geared toward improving communication with your team. Communication has to be the cornerstone of your team. You may have heard the phrase, "The left hand did not know what the right hand was doing." It is not only within the team that there needs to a clear line of communication, but also between leaders and those under the leaders. A manager may have wonderful ideas about how a project should go, but if he does not know how to communicate those ideas to the team, then the ideas will remain on the drawing board and never see their full potential.

Let us look at our symphony again. The conductor has to communicate to the orchestra what he wants to happen. First, the conductor has in his head what the music should sound like. Then, he has to translate that into words and actions that the orchestra can understand. There are accepted terms that both the musician and the conductor know. When the conductor says that the orchestra must "crescendo" in measure 100 of a piece of music, then the orchestra members know that "crescendo" means to get louder. They even write a symbol under measure 100. When they get to this part of the music they know that that symbol means get louder. To further emphasize the point, the conductor may use one of his hands and gradually lift it into the air at measure 100. The musicians know that this nonverbal communication means to get loud. Without communication, either verbal or nonverbal, nothing would happen differently in measure 100.

Let us suppose the musician did not know what the word meant. He probably would not write it on his music and, when he came to that part in the music, would not get louder. The conductor tried to communicate this idea, but they did not share a common language. There is a breakdown in communication. If the musician does not know what the hand motion means, then the idea in the conductor's head cannot become a reality.

This brings us to another important point. If there is not an agreement on what the terms are during communication, then communication and understanding cannot occur.

For effective communication to occur, the other party must be actively listening and paying attention. In addition a manager must also be willing to actively listen to what the team member has to say. Here is a list of things that can help clear, active listening occur:

- Make sure you have enough time to discuss whatever the issue may be. If there is not enough time, try to set up a better time to talk. A team member will feel insignificant if you rush them and look at your watch. You might miss key issues if you do not have the time to give your full attention.

- Pay attention to where you are trying to have a conversation. Is it quiet enough? Are there distractions? Are there others around that may not need to be a part of the conversation? If you need to adjourn until you can find a location more conducive to clear communication, then do so.

- Try to understand the person first before you try to interject your point of view. You cannot talk and listen at the same time.

- Reframe what the person has just said to you. This means that you repeat what they said in your own words. The person will feel like you are really listening to them. It also allows you the opportunity to truly understand what they are trying to communicate and what their point of view is.

- Try not to think about what you are going to say next. Understand what the person is trying to tell you and then, when you feel that you understand and they verify that you understand, you should give point of view. If you have truly listened to the other person, your point of view may transform into something that is closer to what your team member's point of view is.

- Eye contact is important. This builds trust and a feeling of mutual respect.

2

Which Activities Are a Better Fit for Your Team?

You must understand the culture of an organization very well in order to make an assessment of what type of activities will work to foster teambuilding. How well does management communicate vision and purpose to the workforce? Are your managers and supervisors reinforcing a common purpose and rewarding progress towards that goal, or are they sending negative messages to the workforce? Are your managers and supervisors so overwhelmed with day to day tasks that they don't have time to communicate and build team spirit? What is your employee to manager/supervisor ratio? While the ideal ratio varies depending on the complexity of the jobs and the type of business, it is not a recipe for team success to have too few supervisors to effectively facilitate teamwork and positive communication. For less skilled jobs, it is ideal to have no more than about 20 employees for one supervisor, while that number is somewhat lower for highly skilled jobs.

I mention this because it does no good to have a teambuilding activity, and then have the employee go back to a situation where there is one supervisor for 100+ employees. I have worked in companies in which the supervisors were so overwhelmed with just keeping the production lines running that there was no time to reinforce and build on lessons that may have been learned from a team activity two months earlier.

Evaluate how you define the supervisor and manager roles in your company. If your supervisor roles are designed to get product out the door and nothing else, and you provide no training and no time for team activities, your organization will fail to create a true team culture. If necessary, realign the role of your management toward creating a team culture, along with productivity of the department. If you have supervisors and managers who do not have positive communication skills, you will have to design a training and mentoring program to improve those skills, and be willing to, if necessary, remove individuals who are not capable of facilitating a team culture.

Stephen Coenen

Making sure that you have chosen the right activities to do with your team is important. If you do not spend the time to evaluate what your team really needs, you may be wasting your time and money. The orchestra is all about teambuilding all the time. One of our former members (a string section leader) commented that this was the happiest orchestra she had ever worked in. That was a message I enjoyed receiving, because it meant that the players felt invested in the product.

John Gordon Ross

Some team members may feel awkward or feel that it is a waste of time for the team and organization to do teambuilding activities. Actually the contrary is true.

If you do not take the time to build a strong team, time will be wasted and work will be less efficient. There are some team members who may be afraid or uncomfortable with teambuilding activities. Buy-in has to start at the management level. If there is not a firm commitment to changing and improving the team and a belief that the activities will help facilitate and bring about these changes, then the group may be wasting their time.

The team looks to the leader for guidance and the leader sets the tempo for the group. If the leader makes comments about the activity being a waste of time, the team members will more than likely follow suit.

If, on the other hand, the leader makes statements about how the work is important and that everyone will be expected not only to participate in the teambuilding activities but also to implement what they learned, then the team will be on the road to long-term success.

Pramod Goel recommends that team leaders do the following in order to assess the teambuilding needs of an organization:

- Interviews with all involved: Senior management, mid-management, and individual contributors

- Observation: Walk around, water cooler discussions, random process observation, etc.

- Surveys: Generate a baseline survey to benchmark current sentiments of the people involved or impacted

- Focus Groups: Create focus groups to understand underlying issues

Exercises must be appropriate for what the team does, as well as the particular area that the team needs work on. Also make sure you use an exercise that is for the right size of your company.

I tend to think of group activities in logistics of the group. How many are in the group? Would the exercise work better if you split everyone into smaller groups? What is the general physical condition of the group?

Many activities can be physical; can the group get on the floor for some tasks? What are your immediate time constraints; should you only have one exercise, or do you have time for a round of exercises? If the group feels comfortable, then the exercise will go well.

Then, consider what you want to accomplish with the activity. Is this a group of people who have known each other for a long time or for a short time? How long will the group stay together after the event?

Does the group need assistance with communication skills, trust issues, or overall group problem solving skills? Almost all activities can incorporate these skills, so any wrap-up activity should focus on what you wanted the group to get out of the activity.

You should always allow space for the activity to take on a life of its own. You may go into it thinking the group will get one lesson out of it. If they walk away with a totally different lesson learned, do not count it as a wash. You will not always be able to see all possible outcomes, but if you give the group room to play, things that need to float to the top will do so.

Michelle Lovejoy

For groups new to each other, basic teambuilding activities focused on learning names, interests, and experiences will help form the group. Groups that are well-established will also benefit from basic teambuilding activities focusing more on the fun of reconnecting with each other. By observing the interaction of the group during basic activities, the focus can be steered to address specific concerns (communication, leadership, ways of work, etc.) There are teambuilding activities for all types of groups.

Deb Dowling

Sometimes it is hard to know what type of activities would help a group. A group or team leader may merely have a sense that the team is not working together as efficiently and effectively as they could. In this case, just trying an activity together is important.

If a team leader feels that the team members are not working together well, then the team leader should pick an activity that makes the team members work together. For instance, tell everyone that they are stuck on a mountain top (or any other location that is interesting) together. They have to find a way down the mountain, but they can't lose anyone on the way. Every single person has to be at the bottom of the mountain together at the end of the exercise. Then, give one or two people specific handicaps that limit their mobility: One person cannot use his arm while another person can't use one of her legs. These handicaps will force others to help those in need: They all have to work together to successfully complete the exercise.

Kim Stinson

Goals and Common Purpose

Many of the activities in the next chapter assist a team in getting to know each other and to begin working together as a functioning unit.

The team must understand their connection to the larger organization in which they reside. They must understand what it is that their team is supposed to be doing and why the team exists. Once they know what their purpose is they must have a clear understanding of what work they are supposed to be doing and how that work is supposed to be accomplished.

Most teams have a general understanding of why they exist and what they are supposed to do. Good teams go beyond these simple understandings. A good team develops its own ethics and common values. This creates trust among members of the team because they know what is expected of them and that the expectations are the same for everyone else.

The other component of an excellent team is a form of evaluation. This means that, as the team works together, they can continuously evaluate where there are weaknesses and identify and celebrate successes. Once areas are identified that need to be improved, you can use the exercises in this book to help develop strategies and solutions to the areas that need work.

3

Getting Acquainted &
Teamwork Activities

Teambuilding activities bring play into the workplace. Play is the earliest method of learning and simple group projects can help a group learn a way of thinking together.

Michelle Lovejoy

Your team should decide when a good day would be to have teambuilding exercises. This should be a fun and casual day that you can use as a retreat. The time spent on teambuilding exercises will only increase productivity, morale, and teamwork within your organization. If the administration says they cannot do without you for a whole day, do at least a half day retreat.

At your planning meeting decide on a place, time, and other details, such as food. Nothing brings a team together more than eating together. People can show off their signature recipes. If you do not have the room or the time, pick a restaurant that the majority of the team can agree on. Plan enough in advance so people can make the necessary arrangements, and if other teams need to cover for you, they can make arrangements. Planning ahead at least two weeks is a good rule of thumb.

Decide on a place where you will be comfortable and have plenty of room. It is sometimes a better idea not to have your teambuilding retreat at the place you work. Getting away from the office helps change people's mindsets and allows everyone to relax and be more open and genuine. This is a very important key in effective teambuilding activities.

Some venues you might consider

- A coworker's home. If it is big and comfortable enough, this can work. Make sure everyone stays afterward to clean and that this is not an imposition on a coworker — just because they have a pool and jacuzzi does not mean they are obligated to host the teambuilding retreat.

- A hotel conference room. You may need to shop around, as this can be a little pricey. However, some places charge by the hour.

- Some restaurants and coffee houses have an extra area or conference room. Make sure there is enough room to move around and do activities. Ask the management if you would be disturbing other customers. Some places may be too loud and distracting, so check out the venue first before making a decision.

- Libraries often have rooms you can use and would be large enough to accommodate you. The best thing is that these rooms are usually free. They book up quickly so plan well in advance.

- Parks have picnic shelters you can reserve, sometimes for free. These usually have greater availability during the week. Think of an alternate rain site if you are going to have your teambuilding retreat outdoors.

- Churches. These are a great resource and are often free if a team member belongs to the congregation.

- Club houses at apartment complexes are a great place if a member of your team lives at that particular complex. This usually includes access to a pool when the activities are over.

- Your local YMCA or YWCA might have rooms you can use. Again this is usually only an option if a member of your team has a membership.

Companies and organizations have to realize that, to achieve maximum results, people have to be able to trust and work together as a team. We have all seen examples of sports teams that spend a lot of money signing very talented players, but end up not doing very well on the field, because not enough effort and resources are used to help this group of talented individuals find a common purpose above and beyond personal achievements. The team suffers as the individual players go after scoring a lot of points or making themselves look better. As Jeff Van Gundy once said, "To win a championship, a player must be willing to give up money, playing time, or personal statistics, and often must give up all three of those things."

An organization, whether a large pharmaceutical and health care company (where I now work) or a nonprofit that is trying to feed the poor, must cultivate a larger purpose and meaningfulness to their activities, and give people the time, tools, and resources to be able to work in synergy with one another to achieve a larger goal. Without a common purpose by all people on a team, from the CEO or President all the way down to the janitors, people will tend to favor their own interests at the expense of others or the organization, the people will have a lower commitment to the organization, and the organization will not achieve its goals. This is not because people are greedy or inherently self-centered, but if the organization does not foster a culture that supports a central goal, and does not give the people the time and resources to develop a true sense of common identity, it is natural for a person to protect their own interests first, and worry about the organization's goals later.

Stephen Coenen

Be creative, but plan ahead. Make sure you have an agenda worked out, and give this to the team members before the day of the teambuilding retreat. In the agenda make sure you figure in breaks and time to eat. Make the dress casual, but encourage people to wear loose clothing because they will be up and moving around. This is a good opportunity to give members of the team task roles. This gives each team member a sense of being a part of the team, and it also spreads responsibility of planning so the entire project does not rest on your shoulders alone. As the day approaches, check in with your team members to make sure all the preparations are in place.

The remainder of this chapter will have exercises specifically geared toward teamwork. In the next chapter you will find games and activities focused on communication skills in the team.

Before You Begin a Teambuilding Session

Here is a checklist of tasks to complete before you begin each session of teambuilding exercises:

- Make sure you have enough time for the activities. If you are racing against the clock, schedule the teambuilding activities for another day. If you rush through an exercise, you are not only wasting time and money, but you are setting the tone for future teambuilding sessions. Team members will not take the activities seriously because you have not made them a priority. Each of the exercises has a time that it takes to complete, as well as the time required to set up each activity.

- Schedule breaks. You are working with humans, not machines. They need breaks to go to the bathroom, and they need a mental break. People have about an hour long attention span before their minds begin to wander. If you are working with children, their attention spans are even shorter.

- Make sure that you have water and snacks. People do better when they are hydrated. Avoid sodas and sweet snacks. These can cause some people to fall asleep after a short burst of energy. Fruit and protein foods, like peanut butter, are better and healthier choices.

- If you are doing a day-long teambuilding session, make sure that you have planned lunch. I recommend that you bring food in. If people leave for lunch, they may be late getting back and they may have discussions about the activities that may be better within the larger group. Some team members can negatively influence others, and the whole mood and energy level can die after lunch. If you have lunch brought in, you can make it a working lunch. You can give team members an assignment for an activity after lunch or you can have a group discussion about the activities they have already accomplished. You can also have a guest speaker come in to teach a new teambuilding skill or concept. If they do have lunch on their own, have a few places that they can go. Encourage the team members to go in groups to build rapport.

- Look over the activities you have chosen. Double check that you have all the supplies you need for each activity. Have a couple back-up activities ready in case you need them. You may have extra time or a particular activity may not work as expected.

- Look over the space you are using. Make sure you have everything in place for the activities you have chosen. If you need help setting up, make sure that you have planned this ahead of time. There are a few room setups that work well with these activities.

  - Have tables in a "U" shape. That way it will give you plenty of room in the middle of the area to do activities. It also allows you to interact with all the team members at once. If you need more room, it is easier to just push tables and chairs backward in this configuration.

  - Have chairs set up in a circle. In this configuration everyone is equal and important. It gives a sense that no one is above anyone else and the team is in it together.

  - Have no chairs in the room. This is beneficial when you need a larger space to do activities. People can sit in a circle on the floor. Make sure everyone is in optimum health if you choose this configuration, as some people may have difficulty getting up and down.

- If you choose an outdoor setting, make sure you bring chairs or have each team member bring a chair.

- This may seem obvious, but do not allow people to drink alcohol during the teambuilding sessions. Some groups are very close and enjoy socializing. There is a time and place for these sorts of activities and teambuilding time is not one of them. I had the experience of having a daylong team retreat that was scheduled to take place at a bar. As you might guess, not a whole lot was accomplished that day. If you choose to meet afterward to socialize, that is fine as long as it occurs after the scheduled teambuilding activities. You may wish to mention that people should not drink during the lunch hour, as your afternoon sessions may not go as well.

- If there are smokers in the group, make sure they have a designated place and time to smoke (during breaks).

- Make sure that, if anyone on the team has special needs, accommodations are made ahead of time. Pick activities that are not only age appropriate for your team, but that also take into account any member that cannot participate. There are 365 activities in this book to choose from. If a team member is sitting on the sidelines watching, the whole point of teambuilding can be destroyed.

- Make sure to tell people to dress in loose, comfortable clothing. Some of the activities can be physically challenging, and team members need to dress appropriately. If your organization has a dress code, make sure you get permission for your team to dress down that day.

- Try to remove any and all distractions. That means you may have to check cell phones, PDAs, and pagers at the door. Make sure that team members have cleared their calendar during the time you have scheduled for teambuilding. Nothing can break a group's concentration more than ringing cell phones.

• Consider giving rewards for correct answers to queries and active participation. These can be small candy rewards or some cheap toys to play with like clay or colored pens. They can be motivational rewards like time off from work or a pass to dress down for a day. Rewards can be motivational, but at the same time distracting. You are the best judge of your group and how they would react to small prizes and awards.

Each activity in this book has a number of components to help you set up and play each game. Here are descriptions of each:

1. **Name of the game:** This describes what the theme of the game is.

2. **Purpose:** This describes what type of game it is. These can range from getting acquainted games to communication games. The purpose describes briefly what the team should get out of the activity.

3. **Group size:** This describes the right size of team for the activity. Too many or not enough people can make a game difficult or impossible to play.

4. **Level:** This describes how in depth the particular game goes.

   A. 1st: This level is a good ice-breaker activity used with people who may not know each other or have not worked together very long. These types of activities are usually short and fun. These activities are commonly done as the first activity.

   B. Basic: This is an activity with a group that has worked together a while. These build basic teambuilding skills. They are used to teach and explore basic principles. These activities do not usually evoke emotional responses.

C. Advanced: The team leader should consider this level carefully, as these activities are usually more complex. They deal with more serious issues and can evoke some intense discussion and emotional responses. These are recommended for groups that have been working together a while and have done a number of basic exercises because advanced games build upon skills that have already been learned and that are working.

5. **What do you need?** This describes what materials are needed to complete the task. It may give suggestions for the area in which the game needs to be played and gives the leader instructions about what do ahead of time to prepare for the activity.

6. **How much time does it take?** This describes how long a game or activity should take. In some cases it will also give the leader an estimate about how much preparation time is needed.

7. **Description:** This gives a detailed explanation of the game, how it is played, and what the rules are. It may also contain information about what the team should learn by completing the game. There may be other versions of the game in italics below the main description. These may be other variations on the game, including advanced level versions of the game.

8. **Alternate or Advanced Versions:** These require that you look at the original version for guidance. These versions of the exercises need other materials, may create a greater challenge, or may be a more advanced exercise. They are similar but not the same as the original, so read them carefully. These are exercises that add on to more basic versions.

Get Acquainted and Teamwork Games

1. **Who Am I? (TV Character)**

   Purpose: Getting to know each other

   Group Size: 3+

   Level: 1st/Basic

   What do you need? Tape, paper, pen

   How much time does it take? 5 to 10 minutes

   Description: Put the name of a TV character on the back of each member. Each individual will try to determine what TV personality is on his/her back by asking the other team members questions. The person who guesses the name of the character first wins.

2. **Who Am I? (Biography)**

   Purpose: Getting to know each other

   Group Size: 5+

   Level: 1st/Basic

   What do you need? Index cards, pens for everyone, a list of team members for each player

   How much time does it take? 10 to 15 minutes (5 to 10 minutes of prep time)

   Description: Each person fills out a brief bio form prior to the game. The leader needs to allow about 5 to 10 minutes for team members to fill these out. Include interesting facts about yourself that other members of the group do not know. All members must hand back their bio sheets when the meeting begins. The leader will assign a number to each of the index cards handed in. The leader will hand out the sheet with a list of the members. This list helps the members get to know each other's names and it provides a scratch sheet for the team members to make notes on as the game progresses. The team leader then reads off the number and information on each of the cards. The team members write down on their list who they think it is. The member who is able to accurately identify fellow team members wins.

3. **Who Am I? (Embarrassing Moment)**

    Purpose: Getting to know each other

    Group Size: 5+

    Level: 1st/Basic

    What do you need? Pens, index cards

    How much time does it take? 5 to 10 minutes (5 minutes of prep time)

    Description: Members are asked to write their most embarrassing moment on index cards and hand them in. The leader should give about five minutes for the team members to write. The leader collects the cards and then reads them off. The members guess whose moment each is; the one who guesses the most accurately wins.

4. **Who Am I? (Favorite Job)**

    Purpose: Getting to know each other

    Group Size: 5+

    Level: 1st/Basic

    What do you need? Pens, index cards

    How much time does it take? 5 to 10 minutes (5 minutes of prep time)

Description: Members are asked to write a brief description of the favorite job they have held. The members hand their cards in to the leader. The leader then reads them off. The one who matches the most team members and jobs wins. This exercise can be used as a prequel exercise to further discussion about building a better team.

5. **Who Am I? (Favorite Class)**

    Purpose: Getting to know each other

    Group Size: 5+

    Level: 1st/Basic

    What do you need? Pens, index cards for each team member

    How much time does it take? 5 to 10 minutes (5 minutes of prep time)

    Description: Members write their favorite class in school. This can be from grade school, high school, or college. The members hand in the cards and the leader reads them off. The one who has the most accurate guesses about which class matches which team member wins.

6. **Who Am I? (Biography)**

    Purpose: Getting to know each other

    Group Size: You need an even number, as this exercise uses pairs. The leader can make up the even number if needed.

    Level: 1st/Basic

    What do you need? Paper, pens

    How much time does it take?: 20+ minutes (10 minutes of prep time)

Description: Members are paired off and sit facing each other. By asking questions of the other, each writes a biography of his or her partner. The leader should give 10 minutes for this part of the activity. After 10 minutes, the leader has the members regroup, and each member will then introduce their partner to the group. This is a good activity for a newly formed team.

7. **Who Am I? (Family Tree)**

   Purpose: Getting to know each other

   Group Size: 5+

   Level: 1st/Basic

   What do you need? Index cards, pens

   How much time does it take? 5 to 10 minutes (5 minutes of prep time)

   Description: Each member writes a description of his or her family. This list includes father, mother, brothers, sisters, etc. The leader collects the cards and reads each aloud. The member who matches the family description with the team member the most times accurately wins.

8. **Personality Types**

   Purpose: Getting to know each other

   Group Size: 5+

   Level: 1st/Basic

   What do you need? A personality type list, descriptions of personality types

   How much time does it take? 10 to 20 minutes (prep time depends on how long it takes leader to find a list of personality types)

Description: The leader should find standard personality type descriptions (look on the Internet or find a book about personality types). The leader will circulate the list of personality types and descriptions. Each team member will determine which type he or she fits and will report to the team with examples that support his or her choice.

9. **Personality Types Advanced Version**

    Description: This variation has team members that have been working together on a regular basis type each other. The leader must decide if this type of activity is right for his team. A sense of humor is needed or feelings could get hurt.

10. **Scavenger Hunt**

    Purpose: Getting to know each other, getting to know the company, and getting to know how to get around the company. This is a teamwork activity.

    Group Size: At least two teams of four

    Level: 1st/Basic

    What do you need? A list of items around the company. This activity needs to be performed where the team works.

    How much time does it take? 30+ minutes (prep time depends on how long it takes the leader to go around the company and make a list of items to find)

    Description: The leader must go around the building and find different items to add to the list. The list should be no longer than 10 items or you may not see the team members the rest of the day. Items that can be considered:

    - Newspaper from 6 months ago
    - Bio of first president of the company

- Number of employees in the company currently

- Year company was founded

- Board members and their occupations

- Bio of current president

- Where the extra ink cartridges are kept

- Where the copy paper is kept

- Where office supplies are kept

- Hidden items, such as a Pez dispenser (these are placed by team leader; they should be in plain sight)

- Fire evacuation plan drawing

- Fire extinguisher (you can put a number of these to find)

- Number of telephones

- Number of outside doors

- Number of windows

- Mission statement

As a team leader you can be creative. This is a great orientation exercise, as members can find their way around while finding materials and objects they may need working at a company. Make sure you let other people in the building know that this is going on. Tell team members not to disturb others while they are working. You could do this exercise during lunch hour or after hours.

Divide your members into teams of 4. Give each team the list of items to find and a time limit. At the end of time, the teams can have show-and-tell, including where items were found. The team with the most items found wins.

11. **Double Jeopardy Ping-Pong**

Purpose: Getting to know each other and rapport building, teamwork

Group Size: At least 2 teams of 2

Level: 1st/Basic

What do you need? Ping pong table, 4 ping pong paddles, 1 or 2 ping pong balls. You also need enough room to play the game. You can go to a game room, or set up your own tables.

How much time does it take? 10 to 20 minutes (prep time involves setting up the table and making sure that there is nothing around that could get broken)

Description: In this activity you run ping-pong doubles tournaments in which partners have their right and left hand bound together. This promotes teamwork and breaks down barriers. As a leader you might consider putting pairs together who usually do not work together.

12. **Show Time**

Purpose: Getting to know each other, and being able to give and receive feedback

Group Size: 4+ (enough to create 2 teams)

Level: 1st/Basic

What do you need? At least 1 video camera — 2 video cameras are preferred

How much time does it take? 20 to 30 minutes. This can be longer if you have only one camera.

Description: The team is split into 2 small teams. Each team will use a video camera and create a 5-minute show. It can be drama, news, think-panel on a topic, or whatever they choose. If there is only 1 video camera, the teams will have to take turns. Give each team 15 to 20 minutes to create their video. The first part of the exercise is for them to pick a topic and then gather props that are handy. As the leader, keep them on track and on time.

After they have created their movie, bring the teams together for show time. You could have popcorn and soda ready for them. Have each team discuss the experience and why they chose their topic.

13. **Showtime Advanced Version**

Description: Have them pretend they are movie critics after the show. Keep it light and fun so no feelings are hurt. The purpose is to give feedback to other coworkers in an appropriate way.

14. **Dinner on a Budget**

Purpose: Getting to know each other, and a teamwork activity

Group Size: 4+

Level: 1st/Basic

What do you need? An agreed upon amount of money for two teams to buy food and kitchen tools — pots, pans, utensils.

The company can supply the money or each team member can agree to donate a few dollars for the game.

You need to have a place to cook and eat that can accommodate 2 teams.

How much time does it take? 2 to 4 hours

Description: The team leader gives each team an agreed upon amount of money. They cannot supplement the money they have received, but they can beg for or borrow food or other items, such as seasonings. Give them a set amount of time to gather the food items and create a menu (no more than about an hour). The two teams will then be given a set amount of time to create their menu. Both teams will share the food created. You need to have a kitchen or maybe 2 that can accommodate 2 teams cooking at once. If you need 2 kitchens, have an agreed upon time to bring the team back together to eat. As the team leader, you need to make sure the teams stay on task and stay on time. Also make sure you have plates and eating utensils as well as a place to eat.

15. **Dinner on a Budget Advanced Version #1**

    Description: In this version you pull out two of the team members and yourself to be judges. After the teams finish their food preparation, the food is presented to the judges, like on Iron Chef. The judges declare one team the winner. This is a good exercise in giving and receiving feedback. In the end everyone wins because they get to eat.

16. **Dinner on a Budget Advanced Version #2**

    Description: If you want to make the game even more like Iron Chef, pick a food ahead of time that has to be used in the dishes created. This promotes creativity and thinking out of the box.

17. **Writing the Future**

    Purpose: Getting to know each other

    Group Size: 3+

    Level: 1st/Basic

    What do you need? Pens, paper

    How much time does it take? 20 minutes (this can be done ahead of time and members can bring their reports to the meeting)

    Description: Members are asked to think about where they will be in ten years, focusing on the following: Job, Residence, Appearance

Have team members bring their reports to the teambuilding meeting and discuss the projections and what it felt like to think in those terms. Leader should give the team time to respond to each person's report.

18. Writing the Future Advanced Version

Description: Members can bring a picture they have either drawn or a photo they have altered by using a pen or manipulating it in a photo program to show what they might look like in ten years. The leader of the group can collect pictures of the team members and put them on display. This helps the members laugh, relax, and take feedback in a positive manner.

19. The Cake Walk

Purpose: Getting to know each other

Group Size: 20+

Level: 1st/Basic/Advanced

What do you need? An area large enough to move around in. Chairs and tables should be cleared from the playing area.

How much time does it take? 5 to 15 minutes

Description: The leader calls out various numbers. This will depend on the size of the group. Numbers from 2 to 8 are probably a good range to work in. The leader plays recorded music while the team members talk and interact with one another. The leader stops the music and shouts out a number. The team members then try to get in groups of that number. For instance, if the leader calls out 3, then the team members will run and get into groups of 3. Whoever is left over must stay outside the playing area. This process is repeated until a small group is left as the winners.

20. **The Cake Walk Advanced Version**

     Description: You can use different characteristics along with the numbers. Following is a list of suggestions:

     - Age

     - Hair color

     - Eye color

     - Clothing color

     - Shoe color

     - Number of children

     - Number of years at the company

     - Favorite restaurant

     - Favorite movie

     An example of what the leader might say is: "Groups of three people who are wearing the same color shoes."

     This exercise will help members of the group get to know more about each other because they have to talk to each other and figure out if they have things in common.

21. **The Name Game**

     Purpose: Getting to know each other

     Group Size: 5+

     Level: 1st/Basic

     What do you need? Name tag stickers, pens. You need enough room to play this game. Chairs and tables should be out of the way.

     How much time does it take? 5 minutes

Description: Each person writes his or her own name on a tag. The leader then collects all the names and the team sits in a circle. The leader then sticks the tags on the backs of the people at random. When the leader says, "go," everyone gets up and tries to find their tag. Each person also tries to prevent others from seeing the tag that is on their back. When team members find their tags, they grab them, and put them on their chests. The game ends when everyone has found his or her tag.

22. **The Great Hunt**

Purpose: Teamwork

Group Size: 4+ (you need pairs or larger groups for this activity)

Level: 1st/Basic

What do you need? Bags. This activity takes place at the company or an area where items can be collected.

How much time does it take? 30+ minutes

Description: Each team is given a bag. They are instructed to gather items that begin with different letters of the company's name. For example: If your company is named "The Fried Fish Company," you would need to find items that begin with the following letters. Some letters you would have to find more one item for.

F = 2 items	R = 1 item	I = 2 items	E = 2 items
D = 2 items	S = 1 item	T = 1 item	C = 1 item
O = 1 item	M = 1 item	P = 1 item	H = 2 items
A = 1 item	N = 1 item	Y = 1 item	

That is a total of 19 items. For example, for "P" you might collect a pencil.

There should be a time limit on the activity. Whoever can bring back the most items in the allotted time wins. You may want to set rules about disturbing others.

23. **The Great Hunt Alternate Version**

Description: This is the same as the basic version rules. In this version you can choose different words and use their letters.

24. **Four Square**

Purpose: Getting to know each other

Group Size: 15+

Level: 1st/Basic

What do you need? A large room broken up into 4 squares with a number marked in each; tape; die or similar method to randomly pick numbers; a list of 20 questions and 4 different answers

How much time does it take? 10 to 15 minutes (prep time 10 to 15 minutes)

Description: The leader divides and marks the room ahead of time. The leader will have a sheet of questions and 4 possible answers. Here is an example:

What flavor of ice cream do you like?

1. Vanilla   2. Chocolate

3. Strawberry   4. Chocolate Chip Cookie Dough

When a question and the answers are read then the members find which square fits their answer. The leader then picks a number by rolling a die or similar method; the number should be 1 through 4. Whatever number is picked, those team members must sit down. The game is played until only a couple of people remain.

Here are some suggested questions:

- Favorite food
- Favorite car
- Favorite movie
- Favorite actor/actress
- Favorite color
- Favorite season
- Favorite holiday

25. Four Square Advanced Version

Description: You can pick questions that are more in-depth.

What is your learning style?

1. Visual　　　　　　2. Verbal

3. Tactile　　　　　　4. Auditory

These questions present a nonthreatening way for members to learn about each other and how they prefer to interact and learn from one another.

26. Name That Balloon

Purpose: Getting to know each other, learning names of team members

Group Size: 10+

Level: 1st/Basic

What do you need? Balloons, paper, pens

How much time does it take? 5 minutes

Description: The team is split up into 2 or more smaller teams. Each person puts his or her name on a piece of paper, slides the piece of paper into the balloon and then blows it up. A person is chosen to be first in each team. The teams get into small circles and place the balloons in the middle. The selected person chooses a balloon and pops it. He takes the name and calls it out, and the person whose name is called comes and pops another balloon. The rule is that people cannot use their hands or feet to break the balloon. The team that pops all balloons first wins.

27. **Whose on Base?**

Purpose: Getting to know each other

Group Size: 8+

Level: 1st/Basic

What do you need? Bases, or choose items that can be used as bases. The number of bases has to be one less than the number of team members.

How much time does it take? 10+ minutes

Description: This is a good ice-breaker activity. The bases are put into a circle. A team member is chosen as the first person to go. That person stands in the middle of the circle. Everyone has one foot on his or her base. The person in the middle calls out a particular item that he or she is wearing or something that applies to him or herself. Here are examples:

- White shoes
- Black hair
- Grandchildren
- Drives a truck
- Ate ice cream this week

It can be anything. If what the person in the middle shouts applies to members on their bases, those members must run and find another base to put their foot on. The person in the middle is also trying to get to one of those bases. One person will be left when everyone is on a base. This person becomes the new caller and must choose something different. The game can continue this way until the leader stops the game.

28. Blind Leading the Blind

Purpose: Getting to know each other, teambuilding and trust-building

Group Size: 8+ (must have an even number)

Level: 1st/Basic

What do you need? Blindfolds

How much time does it take? 10 minutes

Description: Team members are paired up. One person puts on a blindfold. The other person will help them to the other side of the room. The rule is that they can only give voice commands. The helpers cannot touch the other person or use any other cues. They spin the person around a couple of times and then tell them where to go. They can help them navigate doors and stairs, but be careful. After the helpers have directed their blind-folded team members to their destination, the partners switch.

Note: Dan Comer, a teambuilding expert and trainer, uses this activity a lot in his trainings. He says that some of the funniest experiences have happened to partners not paying attention while the other person walks into a wall. Ouch! He says it helps build trust and brings down barriers within teams.

29. Untying the Knot

Purpose: Cooperation and teamwork

Group Size: 8 to 10 people (you can split this activity into groups for a competition)

Level: 1st/Basic

What do you need? No materials except a large enough area to move around in. This is a great outdoor activity.

How much time does it take? 5 to 10 minutes

Description: The team gets into a circle. Each members grabs the hand of someone else, but never 2 hands from the same person. When this is completed the group will be in a large knot. The challenge is to untangle without anyone letting go of hands. They can step over, under, twist, or do anything to return to a large circle again. This can be very challenging, but a lot of fun. You will see the leaders come out in the group as they tell the others what to do next.

30. **Shark-Infested Waters**

    Purpose: This exercise emphasizes teamwork and problem solving between team members.

    Group Size: 8+ (if it is a larger group break it into groups of 8 to 10)

    Level: 1st/Basic

    What do you need? Small raft-shaped pieces of cardboard about a foot in diameter, construction paper, fake sharks, two 2-liter bottles of water or soda, islands, and tape

    You can make water out of construction paper or place fake sharks on the floor. You need a large area to move through. Mark off the 2 islands with tape.

    How much time does it take? 20 minutes (10 minutes of prep time)

    Description Give the team enough rafts for every team member minus one. Read them the following story: "You have been stranded on an island. Across the water is another island that contains the drinks you need. You have miniature life rafts that float but cannot move in the water. If you slide them, they will sink into the ocean. In the water are blood thirsty sharks. On the island there are man-eating bunnies. The bunnies will not hurt a group of people such as yourselves so you need to make it to the other island as a group. Once you get your drinks you must bring them back to the first island."

Have them start on one island and place the boats in the water and move them as needed so the entire group can get to the other island, retrieve the drinks, and return to their island. This promotes group thinking and teamwork.

31. **Cross Country Skiing**

   Purpose: Teamwork

   Group Size: 4+ divided into 2 teams

   Level: 1st/Basic

   What do you need? 2 boards, 8 feet in length and about 4 inches wide, different colored cloth strips (they can be bandanas or about that size), large enough area to ski across

   How much time does it take? 15 to 25 minutes

   Description: You give each team two boards or skis and the cloths. You can make the cloths different colors for each team. The rules are that up to half the team may move across the room at a time. They may not slide the skis and they cannot touch the skis with their hands. The first team to get all their members to the other side wins. They must bring the skis back across the snow to pick up more team members.

   Note: There is a trick to this. If the team thinks about it, they can tie their feet to the skis with the cloth. This takes teamwork and team thinking.

32. **The Plastic Cup Pyramid**

Purpose: Teamwork

Group size: Groups of 6

Level: 1st/Basic

What do you need? 1 rubber band per group, six 3-foot pieces of string per group, 6 plastic drink cups per group, a table for each group

How much time does it take? 20 minutes (10 minutes of prep time)

Description: Tie one end of the 6 strings to each rubber band. What you will have is a circle (rubber band) with 6 spokes or rays coming from it. Places the cup face down on the table. Each team is given a rubber band with strings on it and each member holds one string (or two if there are less than 6 members). The challenge is to use the rubber band to pick up the cups and build a pyramid. You cannot use your hands to touch the cups even if they fall onto the floor. The team that can build a pyramid first wins. If you do not have enough to make two teams, you can have your team just do it as a single challenge.

33. **The Stick Challenge**

    Purpose: Teamwork

    Group Size: 6+

    Level: 1st/Basic

    What do you need? A long stick

    How much time does it take? 5 to 10 minutes

    Description: The group stands close and holds out 2 fingers. The leader balances a stick on the outstretched fingers. The challenge is to lower the stick to the ground without dropping it. Sounds simple, does it not? It is a real challenge and may take a team a few attempts to accomplish.

34. 1, 2 Buckle Your Shoe

Purpose: Teamwork

Group Size: 4+

Level: 1st/Basic

What do you need? People's shoes

How much time does it take? 5 to 10 minutes

Description: Everyone takes off their shoes and unties or unbuckles them. The team members sit in a circle. They place the shoes inside the circle. Everyone links hands. The challenge is to get the shoes back on without letting go of each other's hands. If you split the group into teams, they can race to see who finishes first.

35. 1, 2 Untie Your Shoe

Purpose: Teamwork

Group Size: 4+

Level: 1st/Basic

What do you need? Everyone with shoes

How much time does it take? 5 to 10 minutes

Description: This will not work with women wearing skirts or dresses. The group is broken up into teams. Everyone lies down with his or her feet in the air. The first team to untie everyone's shoes in the group without the use of hands wins. Feet cannot touch the ground during this game.

36. **Baby Toss**

   Purpose: Teamwork

   Group Size: 6+

   Level: Basic

   What do you need? Blankets, soft baby doll for each team

   How much time does it take? 5 to 10 minutes

   Description: The teams each have a blanket they hold between them. The object is to toss and catch the doll between the two teams. The leader has the teams get further and further away from each other. No one can touch the doll unless it hits the ground. This takes coordinated teamwork.

   Variation: If you do this outside, you can do it over a net like a volleyball game.

37. **Can We Build It?**

   Purpose: Teamwork and personal responsibility

   Group Size: 4+

   Level: 1st/Basic

   What do you need? Building blocks

   How much time does it take? 5 to 10 minutes

   Description: The leader builds a small structure out of the blocks and has the group analyze it. There is another pile of blocks that contains the same blocks used in the leader's structure. Each member of the team chooses a block until all of them have been chosen. The rules are that each person may only touch their block and the group must make the same structure as the team leader.

If a team member touches a block that is not his own, the group must start over again.

38. Can We Build It? Advanced Version

Description: After the group has seen the structure the leader covers or blocks the view while they recreate it. At the end the leader shows the group the structure again to see how well they did.

39. Group Sculpting

Purpose: Teamwork

Group Size: 4+

Level: 1st/Basic

What do you need? Clay for each team, whistle

How much time does it take? 10 to 20 minutes

Description: Each team is given a lump of clay. The leader will tell the groups an object or a theme that needs to be sculpted. When the whistle is blown the first person in the team begins to sculpt quickly. After 20 seconds the leader blows the whistle and the next person takes the clay and continues sculpting the object. This continues until every team member has had a turn.

40. Group Sculpting Advanced Version #1

Description: Different colored clays can be used and team members have their own colored clay to add to the sculpture.

41. Group Sculpting Advanced Version #2

Description: In this version the teams critique each other's sculptures. Discuss how team members feel about their sculptures being critiqued. Did they honestly critique each other?

42. Group Sculpting Advanced Version #3

Description: In this version, the leader writes down two different objects for the teams to see. Each team is unaware what the other team's theme was. When it is over the teams can guess what the objects are.

43. People Tic-Tac-Toe

Purpose: Getting to know each other

Group Size: Teams of 5 to 8 members

Level: 1st/Basic

What do you need? A dry erase board or blackboard, 30 questions. Draw a large tic-tac-toe board. Create about 30 questions. Here are suggestions:

- Information about individual team members

- Information about the company or organization

- Information about what was supposed to be learned about teambuilding

- Information about the jobs people have

How much time does it take? 10 to 20 minutes

Description: The group is broken up into 2 teams. Each team designates a speaker. The teams take turns trying to win tic-tac-toe by calling out a particular square. The leader asks a question; if the team gets it right, they get the square. If the team gets it wrong, the other team has a chance to get the square by answering it correctly. If you have watched *Hollywood Squares*, you will understand the concept of the game. The team that gets a tic-tac-toe wins.

44. Name Around the Circle

Purpose: Getting to know each other

Group Size: 4+

Level: 1st/Basic

What do you need? Space to make a circle, a number of softballs

How much time does it take? 10 to 15 minutes

Description: One person starts by shaking the hand of the person to their right. That person responds by repeating the first person's name and their name. The second person shakes the hand of the person to their right and repeats, all around the circle. Encourage silly handshake introductions, as long as people say their name. Then, everyone steps back a half step and is given one a softball. They are to call a name and toss the object to the person whose name is called. The second person says the name of the first person, then names a third and tosses. This repeats until the group gets okay with names, then add more balls. Balls should not have to be tossed in any set pattern.

"Name Around the Circle" is a good tool for learning names in a short amount of time. People feel more comfortable with each other on a first-name basis. Also remembering names is a weakness for some people; this gives them a chance to overcome their weakness with the group in a nonthreatening way.

Michelle Lovejoy

45. Raft Flip

Purpose: Teamwork and problem solving

Group Size: 4+ (if you have enough people you can have 2 teams)

Level: Basic

What do you need? Tarp or sheet 5 x 5 feet or larger

How much time does it take? 10 to 15 minutes

Description: Stand a group of people together on a tarp or sheet. Have the team figure out how to flip the raft without anyone falling into the water (touching the floor). This is a good one if you have 2 teams; you can time each other for some healthy competition. The trick is to start with a corner and fold it over the rest of it, with one person moving it as people in turn pick up their feet and shift a little.

46. **Cookie Towers**

    Purpose: Teamwork and an ice breaker

    Group Size: 4+ (2 or more teams)

    Level: 1st/Basic

    What do you need? Sandwich-style cookies. Each team is given the same number of cookies.

    How much time does it take? 5 to 10 minutes

    Description: Divide your participants into groups of 4 to 6. Each group is given the same number of sandwich-style cookies. The goal is to create the tallest tower of cookies that stands for a specific time period.

47. **Death of a Team Member**

    Purpose: Teamwork and team support

    Group Size: 4+

    Level: Advanced

    What do you need? Small pieces of paper, and a room in which people can move safely around in the dark

How much time does it take? 10 to 15 minutes

Description: The leader creates one small piece of paper per team member playing. On one of the pieces of paper a black dot or an "x" is drawn. All the other pieces of paper are blank. Everyone takes a folded piece of paper; the person who gets the black dot or "x" mark becomes the murderer. Turn out all the lights. This can make it very dark so be careful. Everyone wanders around in the dark until they are "murdered" by having the murderer come up to them and whisper to them that they are dead. The game ends when either everyone has been killed or someone figures out who the murderer is and makes a verbal accusation.

The interesting thing about this game was that people started forming alliances with one another in the dark. If someone was murdered several feet away while you were standing next to someone, you knew that the person next to you wasn't the murderer. So, then, the two of you stuck together, even if you didn't like each other when the lights were on. Having that common experience of staying safe during the game helped you have a better working relationship with your ally when the lights were back on and everyone was back to work the next day.

Kim Stinson

---

48. **Fire Drill**

Purpose: Teamwork

Group Size: 3+

Level: Basic/Advanced

What do you need? Paper with different problems or disasters that could occur within the organization. The team leader needs to write them down on folded slips of paper.

How much time does it take? 20 to 30 minutes (10 minutes prep)

Description: Improvisations can be a great way to get everyone laughing or brainstorming about a particular situation. It is hard, though, for people to come up with situations and characters off the tops of their heads, particularly if they are feeling self-conscious. The team leader should think of ideas for situations and characters and put them on individual pieces of paper. When doing the exercise with the team, have them pull the situations and characters out of a hat or bowl. Have the team visualize what is on the paper. Who would be there? Rescue personnel? The people being rescued? Why are they there? Have the group explore those questions through the exercise. Do not let them discuss and plan it before getting up to do it. Each member of your team should go into the improvisational acting out of the situation knowing who he or she is, but no one else knows. This means that they each need to communicate during the improvisation to find out who each of them is and how they can work together to get everyone to safety. The leader should give them a time limit to play out the scene. A new scene and new characters should be chosen next.

49. Invisible Ball

Purpose: Facilitates cooperation between team members

Group Size: 3+

Level: 1st/Basic

What do you need? No materials needed

How much time does it take? 5 to 10 minutes

Description: The person who is picked to start decides on the type of ball that she holds in her hands. The rest of the group should be able to see or imagine the ball, too. The person should define the size and weight of the ball with her movements not by using words, as this is a silent exercise. Is it a baseball? A golf ball? A beach ball? Once the person with the ball has defined the shape, weight, and any other important characteristics through movement, she passes or throws the ball to another person in the circle who then catches the ball. The second person changes it to another ball and then passes it to a third person. This keeps going until everyone has had a chance to create and throw a ball.

50. Comic Strip

Purpose: Getting to know each other exercise, ice breaker

Group Size: 4+

Level: Basic

What do you need? Comic strips, overhead projector and screen (optional), transparencies (optional). Whiteout the talk bubbles above the characters' heads. Make copies and transparencies if you like. Have a different comic for each small group of 2 to 3 people.

How much time does it take? 10 to 15 minutes (20 to 30 prep time)

Description: Each team fills in the bubbles on their comic strip. The team decides what is said. If you are using transparencies, make sure the teams fill it out to share. After they finish, have them share their strips and why they chose what they said in their comic strips.

51. Comic Strip Advanced Version

Description: In this version the team leader picks themes, emotions, or specific situations that the characters are faced with in the comics.

52. Whine About Wine

Purpose: Teamwork, processing

Group Size: 4+, broken up into teams

Level: 1st/Basic

What do you need? Wine list, index cards

Find a wine list that lets you know whether wines are red or white. You can find these online or you can find them in a wine buying magazine. You need at least 10 of each type. Make a master list of wines for each team. Make cards for each wine's name. Try not to use wines that have red or white in the name of the wine. Each team needs a complete deck of wine cards.

How much time does it take? 15 to 20 minutes

Description: Give each group a deck of wine cards. Tell them they have to separate the cards into red and white wines. When they are done give them a master list to see how they did. Discuss what type of process the groups used in determining whether a wine was white or red.

53. Whine about Wine Alternate Version #1

Description: Have the group determine a price list for the wines. They should order them from least expensive to most expensive. Again, have the group discuss what the process was for making their choices.

54. Whine about Wine Alternate Version #2

Description: Turn up the pressure and see how the team works when faced with a deadline. Set a timer. Give a small reward for the team that gets the most correct before time runs out.

55. Team Feud

Purpose: Ice breaker, getting to know team members better

Group Size: 6+

Level: Basic

What do you need? Questionnaires filled out prior, a desk bell, a chalkboard or whiteboard, chairs

How much time does it take? 20+ minutes (30+ minutes of prep time)

Description: This game is similar to the popular TV game show *Family Feud*. Before you play this game, collect the answers to a questionnaire you have created. Try to get as many people as you can to answer the survey. Tally up the 5 most popular answers to be used with the game.

Set up a table with the bell. The person who rings the bell first can try to answer the question. Each team should have chairs set up in a line. As each person has a turn, the other members move up a chair and the person who had a turn moves to the back.

Here is the order of play:

1. Two people come up for the challenge.

2. On the white board write down 5 slots for the correct answers.

3. Ask the survey question. Whoever rings the bell first gets to answer the question first. If correct, you write it down on the board. The two players sit down at the end of the row on their team's side. You ask the next person the same question.

4. If the first person that rings the bell does not answer the question correctly, the opposing team gets a chance to answer

the question. If the opposing team answers it correctly, then they get to play. If the opposing team does not get it correct, then the other team gets to play.

5. If the winning team gets 3 incorrect answers before clearing all the answers on the board, the opposing team gets to offer an answer. If the opposing team is correct, they win. If they answer it wrong, it is a tie. If the winning team gives all 5 answers before 3 incorrect answers, they win.

6. The game is repeated with a new survey question. Whichever team has the most wins is the overall winner.

Here are some sample survey questions:

What is your favorite color?

What is your favorite animal?

What is your favorite place to eat?

What is your favorite food?

What is your favorite holiday?

56. Team Feud Advanced Version

Description: In this version you ask more in-depth questions that are work- or team-related. Here are some examples:

What is your favorite part of your job?

What is your least favorite rule at work?

What is the best part about being a team member?

What is the team's most shining moment?

What is the team's funniest moment?

57. I Never – Team Style

Purpose: Getting to know team members better

Group Size: 4+

Level: Basic/Advanced

What do you need? 10 rewards for each person. The rewards can be poker chips, wrapped candy, pennies, or any item that is inexpensive and that you can easily handle.

How much time does it take? 10 to 20 minutes

Description: This is similar to the game many people played as a child. In this version, it is team-related. A person begins by saying: "I never ..." and then follows this with something they have never done. If other people in the group have not done the same thing, they give the player one item from their pile. You can continue the game as long as you wish.

You may want to set boundaries so that it does not get too personal or off base. You should choose team- or job-related subjects such as:

- Helped another worker

- Offered a team member a ride home

- Left work early

- Took extra time at lunch

- Made personal calls at work

Each person should have a turn. At the end of the game they can eat the candy or cash in their chips for a larger reward. You decide how to handle this part.

58. **Dodge Mallow**

Purpose: Ice breaker and team rapport

Group Size: 4+ broken up into 2 groups

Level: 1st/Basic

What do you need? A bag of marshmallows (regular size, not minis unless you want to make it harder), an area large enough to play, tape. Divide the playing area in half with tape.

How much time does it take? 5+ minutes

Description: This is a great game to start off a teambuilding session or to liven things up when things are getting boring. This is based on the game dodgeball except you are using marshmallows instead of balls. Give each side a few marshmallows and tell them to start.

Each side tries to hit the other side's players with the marshmallows. If they get hit, they must leave the playing area. If a member of their team catches a marshmallow, then a member on the sideline may return. The games ends when an entire team is eliminated.

59. **Dodge Mallow Advanced Version**

Description: In this version, allow your team to pick teams to play the game on their own. You may see some interesting things happen. You may choose to talk to the team about how they felt to be picked and how they felt to be looked over. Also discuss how they decided to split into teams. What was the process? Who were the leaders in the process?

60. **Protect Your Assets**

Purpose: Team rapport, team building

Group Size: 8+

Level: Basic

What do you need? Sticky notes

How much time does it take? 10 to 15 minutes

Description: Pair off people on the team. One will choose to carry the "asset" first. That person gets a sticky note on their back. The object is to try to get the other team's sticky notes while protecting your sticky note (asset). The team left with their sticky intact wins. You can then switch the partner who is carrying the asset. Have a discussion about how people felt to be protected by a team member and also how they felt protecting someone else.

61. **Mummy Wrap**

Purpose: Rapport, creative collaboration

Group Size: 6+ broken into 2 teams or more

Level: Basic

What do you need? Toilet paper

How much time does it take? 10+ minutes

Description: A person is chosen to be the mummy, and they are wrapped in toilet paper. They may be decorated any way the team chooses, such as a lighthouse, a famous movie character, or anything else. When they are complete they can be shown off to the other teams. Make sure you have a camera ready.

62. **Mummy Wrap Alternative Version**

Description: Choose the object or character for the teams. The team that does the best job (judged by you) wins. This gets teams to be creative and work together with a common goal in mind.

63. **Till Death Do Us Part**

Purpose: To build trust, teamwork

Group Size: 4+ separated into pairs

Level: Basic

What do you need? Something to tie people's hands together

How much time does it take? 10+ minutes

Description: Have people tie one of their hands to the hand of a partner. Now the fun begins as you pick different tasks for the partners to accomplish. Here is a list of suggestions:

- Jump rope

- Put a shirt on over their clothes

- Tie their shoes

- Make a meal

64. **Till Death Do Us Part Alternate Version**

Description: Tie all the members of the team together. Everyone will have both hands tied to someone else. Have the team try to do activities as one large unit. Here are some suggestions:

- Create a piece of art

- Get everyone through a door

- Have everyone write their name on a poster

- Make a pitcher of tea and pour a cup for everyone

The activities are endless. The point is for everyone to work as a unit to accomplish a task together.

65. Switch It

Purpose: Team building/cooperation

Group Size: 4+

Level: Basic

What do you need? A narrow object for the team to stand on. Here is a list of ideas:

- Log
- Bench
- A ski
- Board
- A long string
- A meter stick

How much time does it take? 10 to 15 minutes (5 minutes of prep time or less depending on the object)

Description: Everyone stands on the object. The challenge is to get the team to rearrange themselves so they are in the opposite order they began in. The rule is that everyone must stay on the object. If anyone falls off or steps off the team must restart the challenge.

Afterwards discuss with the group how they accomplished the task. Did everyone have to help get it done? Talk to them about personal boundaries and closeness. How did they feel about that?

66. Group Portrait

Purpose: Being creative as a group

Group Size: 4+ (if larger number of people participates, you may want to consider teams)

Level: Basic

What do you need? Various colors of marker, pen, pencil or paint, and a large piece of paper or butcher paper

How much time does it take? 15 to 20 minutes

Description: Pick an order of the group. The first person makes a mark or line on the paper, then it is the next person's turn. The rule is that no one's line or mark can intersect or cross another person's. The goal is to get the group to make a picture together. They should not talk during this exercise. When everyone has had a turn or two, have them name the picture to describe what it is. Afterward, have them talk about the process. Discuss how it felt to be put in a certain order. Discuss how they came up with a title.

67. Group Portrait Alternate Version #1

Description: In this version give the team an animal or object to draw. They can only make one line or mark during their turn.

68. Group Portrait Alternate Version #2

Description: In this version you may need to go around the group a greater number of times. The same rules apply. The object is to draw a group portrait.

69. Mouse Trap

Purpose: Teamwork

Group Size: 6+ in at least two teams

Level: Advanced

What do you need? Materials to make a machine. These are small items such as:

- Marbles
- Toilet paper rolls
- Scissors
- Paper
- Sticks
- Silverware

How much time does it take? 20+ minutes

Description: This exercise is based on the childhood game "mouse trap." The teams should use the items provided to create a machine that, once set in motion, will continue to work without human interaction. For instance a marble could hit a pencil that falls and hits another ball. The team that can create a "mouse trap" that works the longest wins. Have each group show their mouse trap.

Discuss with the group how they worked together. Did some people do the work while others were on-lookers? Was everyone a part of the process? Did some people bring special skills to the task?

70. Mouse Trap Alternate Version

Description: In this version, have each group help the other improve their machine. How did it feel to have others improve your design? Did you feel defensive about their improvements?

71. Team Bocce Ball

Purpose: Teamwork

Group Size: 6+ in at least two teams

Level: Basic

What do you need? A 2-liter bottle filled with water, small balls, cones or objects to mark off the playing area

How much time does it take? 10+ minutes (10 minutes of prep time)

Description: The area is marked off with four cones or objects. 30 by 30 feet is a good size. The bottle is placed in the middle. The teams surround the area. The goal is to get a ball to touch the bottle but not to knock it over. Here are the rules:

1. The players may never enter the playing area

2. The balls can be thrown at anytime

3. A ball may be hit with another ball to knock it away from the bottle

4. A ball may be knocked out of the playing area and reused

5. If the bottle is knocked over, the team that does it loses three points

6. The game ends when no more balls can be used

7. The team with the most points wins

8. Each team is given the same number of balls at the beginning of the game

9. If a person enters the play area, his team loses two points

The leader is the scorekeeper. Discuss how it felt for other team members to compete against you. Did everyone score? How did it feel to get a ball knocked away from the goal? Did other team members help you score?

72. **Drought**

Purpose: Teamwork

Group Size: 4+ (if there are too many people you may need more than one group)

Level: Basic

What do you need? Two cans, water, chalk, four giant rubber bands (these can be found at a craft store, or you can use any long elastic object). This is an outdoor exercise that needs to be played on level concrete.

How much time does it take? 15+ minutes

Description: The leader draws a large circle with the chalk. One of the cans is filled halfway with water and placed in the middle of the circle. The task is for the team to get the can out of the circle and pour the water into the other can outside the circle. They cannot touch the cans with their hands, they cannot enter the circle at any time, and they must use the rubber bands.

Discuss how the group accomplished the goal. How did it feel to have limited resources? How did the group communicate during this exercise? Did anyone lose their temper or become frustrated?

73. Egg Toss

Purpose: Teamwork and creativity in a group

Group Size: 4+ (at least two teams are formed in this activity)

Level: Basic

What do you need? One raw egg for each team and materials to build the egg carrier such as:

- Cotton
- Egg cartons
- Bubble wrap
- Feathers
- Tape

How much time does it take? 20+ minutes

Description: Each group is given an egg and may use any of the materials to build a carrier. They are given a certain amount of time to accomplish their task. The goal is to create a carrier that can be dropped with an egg inside without breaking the egg.

After teams create the carriers, it is test flight time. Have each team drop their carrier from at least eight feet high. The team whose egg does not break wins.

Have the group discuss how they made the carrier and how they worked as a group. How did it feel to win or lose? Was there a consensus in the group about how the carrier should be built?

74. Egg Toss Alternate Version

Description: Have the teams challenge each other by setting the height higher than the other teams until an egg breaks.

75. The Tower of Terror

Purpose: Teamwork

Group Size: 4+ (at least small two teams)

Level: Basic

What do you need? A deck of playing cards for each team, stop watch

How much time does it take? 10+ minutes

Description: Each team is given the challenge of building the tallest tower. Each team member must participate and take turns adding cards to the tower. If it collapses, they must start over. You set a time of 10 minutes. Discuss with the team how they felt in this activity. Did they trust other team members not to knock the tower down? Was it hard to relinquish control to other team members?

76. The Tower of Terror Alternate Version #1

Description: Set the clock to a shorter time. Keep making the time shorter and shorter. Discuss how this reduced time made them feel? Did they get careless?

77. The Tower of Terror Alternate Version #2

Description: Have the teams do the activity with just one hand. Have them start with their dominant hand, and then have them switch to their non-dominant hand. Discuss how this felt. Did it increase their stress?

78. Global Warming

Purpose: Teamwork and problem solving

Group Size: 6+ (at least two teams)

Level: Basic

What do you need? Two large bowls (they must be the same size) and water. This is an outdoor activity.

How much time does it take? 10+ (overnight prep for the ice)

Description: Freeze water in the bowls. Allow them to become solid overnight. If you like to be creative, add some food color for fun. Take the icecaps and put them in a cooler with a lot of ice to keep them frozen. Each team is given one directive: Melt the ice cap before the other team melts theirs.

Each team must figure out a way to melt their ice cap before the other team. Discuss how they solved this task. How did they work as a team? How was the problem process? Was it efficient enough to get the task done quickly?

79. The Funky Clock

Purpose: Teamwork

Group Size: 6+

Level: Basic

What do you need? No extra materials are needed

How much time does it take? 5+ minutes

Description: The team gets into a tight circle with everyone's shoulder touching his or her neighbor's. Now have everyone bend down and reach between his or her legs and grab their neighbors' hands. They will be in an odd position that may not be very comfortable. Now ask the entire team (clock) to rotate clockwise until everyone returns to his or her original position. They cannot fall or let go of their neighbors' hands.

Discuss how the group worked together. Did they communicate with one another? Was it important to rely on other team members to accomplish the task?

80. The Human Wheel

Purpose: Teamwork

Group Size: 5+ (if there is a larger number the team should be broken into smaller groups)

Level: Basic

What do you need? Space large enough to move in

How much time does it take? 5 to 10 minutes

Description: One person stands in the middle of team members in a circle. The object is for the person to grab one foot or leg of every member of the group at the same time. The person in the middle is the hub of the wheel. As a group they must move across the room without the person in the middle dropping anyone's leg or foot. This exercise can be repeated with different people as the hub of the human wheel.

Discuss how people felt being the hub or the spoke in the wheel. How did they work together? Did they discuss what they were going to do before they did the activity?

81. Team Trash Basketball

Purpose: Teamwork

Group Size: 12+ (four teams)

Level: Basic

What do you need? 2 trash baskets, 2 small balls or balls made from wadded paper, name tags for everyone, a board to stick the name tags on

How much time does it take? 10 to 15 minutes (5 to 10 minutes of prep time)

Description: The two waste paper baskets are set up at opposite sides of the room. Each person puts on a name tag. The team leader counts out four teams.

The object of the game is to make sure all the players on your team score a basket before the other teams do. Two teams are assigned to a basket. If a person scores, they must put his or her tag on the board. Once all team members have their names on the board, the team wins. The same person cannot score more than once. The purpose of the game is to help other team members score.

The two games go on at the same time until there is a winner. The opposing teams can block shots and try to stop the other team from scoring. Keep it safe so no one gets hurt! If someone hits someone else, that person can take a foul shot if he has not scored yet (you may need two referees to watch these games).

Discuss how the teams helped each other. How did they feel helping other members score rather than scoring all the points themselves?

82. **Popcorn**

Purpose: Teamwork

Group Size: 4+

Level: Basic

What do you need? A large bed sheet, small balls (like ping pong balls, racket balls, tennis balls), a large enough area to play

How much time does it take? 10+ minutes

Description: Have the team grab the sheet, make it taut, and add the balls on top. One member should shake the sheet and see if he or she can get the balls to pop up and down. Keep adding team members to shake the sheet. The object is to get all of the balls popping at once. Adding more balls increases the challenge.

Discuss with the group how one member could not make it happen. Discuss how the team had to work together to accomplish the task.

83. **Cat's Cradle**

Purpose: Teamwork

Group Size: 4+

Level: Basic

What do you need? A large rope, blindfolds for everyone on the team

How much time does it take? 10+ minutes

Description: The team is blindfolded and the rope is tied end to end and placed at the team's feet. The challenge is to get the team to make a triangle with the rope. When the team thinks they are done, have them look at what they did. You can try a square, octagon, or any other shape.

Discuss with them how it felt to work together to accomplish the task. Did it turn out the way they thought it would?

84. Cat's Cradle Alternate Version

Description: In this version, set up a video camera and tape the exercise. Play the recording back to the team and talk about their interactions and how they could work better as a group. It will be funny, so laughing is acceptable.

85. Snapshot

Purpose: Cooperation, team work.

Group Size: 4+ (you need at least two groups)

Level: Advanced

What do you need? Materials to build at least 3 sculptures. The leader and each team must have the same materials to build the same sculptures. This can be clays, popsicle sticks, glue or whatever material you want to use. Also find something to cover and hide the sculpture.

How much time does it take? 20+ minutes (15+ minutes of prep time)

Description: The leader makes a sculpture before the exercise and neither team can see it. The leader should hide the sculpture in such a way that he can allow one team member from each group at a time can see it. Each group should be far enough away from each other that they cannot see what the other group is doing.

The exercise begins as one member from each team comes and looks at the leader's sculpture. The leader should give them 10 seconds to look at it and memorize it. Then they return to their groups and begin working on their sculptures. After a few minutes, someone different from each team comes and gets a mental snapshot of the sculpture. They return to their groups and continue working on their version of the sculptures. This continues until each member has had a chance to view the sculpture. The leader will then call time. The leader will ask for all the sculptures to be brought to the front and then reveal the actual sculpture. The group will discuss their efforts. How did the vision of the sculpture change as each member of the group had a look at the sculpture? How did it feel to be a part of a group and not have any idea what the sculpture should look like? How did it feel to be the last person to see the sculpture? What did each member contribute to the effort? Did anyone try to draw what he or she saw?

86. Barrel of Monkeys

Purpose: Teamwork, cooperation

Group Size: 4+ (this is a partner activity)

Level: Basic

What do you need? No extra materials are needed

How much time does it take? 5+ minutes

Description: Make sure that everyone has a partner. Have each pair hold out their left hands. Tell them to grab their partners' hands while holding their hands in a "C" shape. Thumbs are not used. It is like the game "Barrel of Monkeys" in that they are just hooking their hands together, not really gripping the other person's hand.

The leader says the following:

"The goal of this exercise is to try to touch your partner's shoulder with your hooked hand. You cannot let go of your partner's hand. Keep count of how many times you touch your partner's shoulder. The most touches win."

The winner is actually the team with the most touches. Give five minutes to complete the exercise. Partners will more than likely work against one another to try to their own partner's shoulder.

The point of the exercise is how people work against one another when trying to accomplish a task, when, if they worked together, they could accomplish it easier. Do not tell them this until they have completed the exercise.

Discuss this exercise with the tem. Why did they work against one another? Were there partners that worked with each other to try to get the most points? What made them decide to do that? Why do partners work against each other in the workplace? What happens when team members work together?

87. **Hop**

Purpose: Teamwork and problem solving

Group Size: 4+ (this exercise may be limited to a smaller group due to the size of the jump rope)

Level: Basic

What do you need? A large jump rope or a number of smaller jump ropes tied together and a large area; this is a good outdoor activity

How much time does it take? 5+ minutes

Description: Two people are chosen to swing the rope. The task is to get everyone on the team to jump once at the same time with the jump rope. They must determine how they will accomplish this. There are a number of ways they can accomplish this activity. There is no right way.

Discuss with the group how they came up with the solution. How did they deal with people who could not jump well? Why was it important for everyone to work together in unison?

88. **Hop Alternate Version**

Description: Challenge the team to jump more than once. You can split up the team for some friendly competition and see which group can jump the most.

89. **The Many Legged Monster**

Purpose: Teamwork and cooperation

Group Size: 6+ (this activity needs at least 2 teams)

Level: Basic

What do you need? 2 taped lines that are parallel and 15 feet from one another

How much time does it take? 15 minutes

Description: The group must go from one line to another as a group. They have touch points on their bodies. A touch point is anything that touches the group. This can be any body part like a leg, arm, or elbow. Once a touch point is used, it cannot be reused and is only counted once. Pick a number of touch points that a group can use to get from one line to another. You can count the number of people and subtract two to three touch points that they can use. For example:

Five people in a group may be allowed to use three touch points. The groups must work together and be creative. The fewer the number of touch points allowed, the harder it will be.

Discuss with the groups how they completed the activity. Was communication important? Were skills and flexibility of individuals considered? Did the group feel uncomfortable being close and possibly having to touch other team members?

90. Water Sports

Purpose: Teamwork and team cooperation

Group Size: 4+

Level: Basic

What do you need? A tray that can hold 10 paper cups, 10 paper cups, water

How much time does it take? 20+ minutes (5 to 10 minutes of prep time)

Description: Fill the cups with water just over half full. Place five of the cups in a row. Thirty feet from away, place the other five cups. Place the tray in the middle. This activity may be better outdoors, as the water may be spilled.

Have the group gather in the center. Tell them that the objective is to grab all ten cups and place them on the tray. They must do this by gathering one cup at a time from each side of the room and must alternate sides as each cup is obtained. They must have all ten cups on the tray and returned to the center. Each team member can use only one foot and one hand at a time. If any water is spilled, they must start over. There are a few different strategies to completing this task, but the team must work together to get it accomplished.

Discuss with the group how they accomplished the task. Was everyone involved? Did they fail a couple of times before figuring out how to do it? Did they start the task without discussing it first as a group? Was everyone involved in the decision making?

91. Waterfall

Purpose: Teamwork and team ingenuity

Group Size: 6+

Level: Basic

What do you need? Whatever is nearby. You can plant some items that can be used.

How much time does it take? 20+ minutes

Description: Mark off a 30-foot chasm on the floor or ground. Have three of the team members go to one side of the waterfall. These are the victims that need to be rescued. The other team members must figure out how to get across the waterfall to get to those who need to be rescued. They must use what is available to them (clothes, socks, a tree limb). They have to throw a safety line across the waterfall for victims to grab. If the line falls into the water, it must be retrieved and the team must try again. They should be able to rescue the victims one at a time.

Discuss with the team how it felt to be a victim. How did it feel to rely on others? How did the group solve the problem? Did the victims offer suggestions? Was it a team effort, or did just a couple of people take over the task? How did it feel to have limited resources?

92. **The Story Tower**

Purpose: Team understanding

Group Size: 4+

Level: Advanced

What do you need? Paper towel tubes for each person, colored pens, paper, glue, scissors

How much time does it take? 60+ minutes

Description: Each person creates a character in a story. The story is about the creation, purpose, and workings of the team. The characters should be different animals or mythical creatures.

When it is completed, the group should create the story using all of the characters. One of the team members will write the story down and the characters should be attached together to make a tower while the story is told.

How did the members feel about the team's creation story? How did it feel to create a character in that story and have it woven into both the story and tower? Was every character important? Could the tower stand without each character? Would the story be different without some of the characters?

93. The Mood Hats

Purpose: Discussion of team feelings

Group Size: 4+

Level: Advanced

What do you need? Many different kinds of hats. You can usually find these at a secondhand or thrift store for cheap.

How much time does it take? 20+ minutes

Description: Place the hats on a table. Pick a member to choose a hat. They are to state why that hat represents them. Each member will have a turn picking a different hat. After they finish, they should return the hat to the table.

Here is a list of other topics the hats can be used for:

- How do you feel about the team?

- How do you wish to see the team?

- Which hat represents the best part of the team?

- Which hat represents the worst part of the team?

Discuss with the team how they felt about wearing the hats. How did they feel about other teammate's responses? Did the responses influence their hat choices? How does a teammate's choice affect other team members?

94. The Mood Hats Alternate Version #1

Description: This is the same as the first version except that masks are used instead of hats. Try to get a variety of different creatures, expressions, and types of masks.

95. The Mood Hats Alternate Version #2

Description: Instead of supplying the hats or masks, have the team members create them to represent the different feelings associated with the group.

96. Team Symbol

Purpose: Group identity development

Group Size: 4+

Level: Advanced

What do you need? A lot of different magazines that can be cut up, a few pairs of scissors, paste, a poster board

How much time does it take? 20+ minutes

Description: Each team member must cut out two pictures from the magazines. One represents the team, the other represents how the person feels about his or her role on the team. After all of the team members have found and cut out their two pictures, they should share what the pictures mean and glue it to the poster board. Each team member then adds his or her picture to the collage. The final picture is the group's symbol.

Discuss with the group how they felt about finding pictures that represented the team. Was it difficult? How do they feel about the final symbol? Is it a good representation of the entire team?

97. The Magazine Awards

Purpose: Team appreciation

Group Size: 4+

Level: Advanced

What do you need? A pile of various magazines, scissors, tape, paper

How much time does it take? 20+ minutes (5 minutes of prep time)

Description: Write down everyone's name on a slip of paper and have the team members pick one of the slips. If they choose their own name, they must return it to the pile. Have the team create a trophy out of the magazines for the person they have chosen. It should reflect the best qualities of that person and what strengths he or she brings to the team. No one should know who is making his or her trophy until the trophies are finished. When the group is finished, they should present the awards and explain them to the team.

The team leader should explore people's feelings about receiving the trophy. How did they feel about making the trophy? Did they find it enjoyable to say something nice about a team member?

98. The Magazine Awards Alternate Version

Description: You can set up an awards ceremony. Have each person present the trophy he or she created to the appropriate person, the person can then come to the front and thank those that made their achievements possible. This activity should reflect the Academy Awards. You can set up a podium and music if you like. A red carpet and formal dress is optional.

99. **Our Forefathers**

Purpose: Team rules

Group Size: 4+ members

Level: Advanced

What do you need? Paper, pens, colored markers, or pencils

How much time does it take? 30+ minutes

Description: The team leader reads the following scenario to the team.

"You have just been notified that you inherited a parcel of land near Alaska. According to the maps, it does not belong to any country and, therefore, is a country unto itself. It is up to the team to create a country from scratch."

Here are the tasks that need to be accomplished. They may take more than one session to complete, so split up the tasks so that they can fit into your time frame. This is a good activity for a multiday teambuilding retreat.

- Country name

- Language of inhabitants

- Monetary system

- System of government

- Main commodity

- Culture

- Main religion

- Political situation with other countries

- Military

- Holidays

- Constitution

- Branches of government

- Voting

- Available food

- Flag

- National bird or flower

100. One Person's Trash Is Another Person's Treasure

Purpose: Team creativity

Group Size: 4+ (at least 2 groups will be formed)

Level: Basic

What do you need? Glue, scissors, any material that would be discarded such as paper towel rolls, string, newspaper, cans, jars, bottles, or magazines

How much time does it take? 20+ minutes

Description: The groups are given a pile of "trash" and use the items to create a masterpiece. Each member of the group must pick an item to add to the piece. When everyone has completed the task, there can be an art show. Each group must describe their art piece.

The leader should ask how it felt to work with others in a creative setting. Was it hard to share and allow others to add to the art piece? Were people surprised by others' creative skills? How was the decision made about what to build and how to build it?

101. **Share the Crayons**

Purpose: Team creativity

Group Size: 4+

Level: Basic

What do you need? Paper, crayons (1 crayon per team member)

How much time does it take? 15+ minutes

Description: Give each team member a different color crayon. Try to have a wide range of colors available. Give the team a subject to draw and color. They must create the object together. Everyone must use his or her own crayon and only one person can draw at a time. The goal is for everyone to use his or her crayon at least once in the picture. You can choose different objects to draw.

The leader can discuss how the group felt about working with others. Was your crayon important? Did you feel needed or did you feel like your crayon was just added because it was the rules?

102. **Share the Crayons Advanced Version #1**

Description: In this version, the team members are timed. The leader has a stopwatch and gives each team member ten seconds to draw his or her part of the picture.

Was it harder to do under a time constraint? Were shortcuts taken? Did the team members feel they had enough time to do their jobs? Did people feel as if they could not complete their job because the previous team members did not complete theirs?

103. **Share the Crayons Advanced Version #2**

Description: In this version, the team members must create two pictures using their crayons. The first is a picture of the team now and the second is a picture of the team in the future. You can decide whether to add time restrictions or not.

When they are finished, they can describe what their picture is and what it means. The team leader can decide to break up the team into two or more groups. Each group can have the same task or separate tasks.

Here are some other versions of the two pictures:

- The team the way it is / The team the way we want it

- The team two years ago / The team now

- The team with everyone working together / The team with everyone not working together

- The team with all the members present / The team with members missing

Discuss with the team how they felt about the different pictures. How did the team go from one picture to the other? Did the team discuss what they were going to draw before they drew it? Did the team draw people or did they draw something else to represent the team?

104. **Big Foot**

Purpose: Teamwork

Group Size: 4+

Level: Basic

What do you need? Old large shoes. You can get some old pairs from a secondhand or thrift store. You need at least 2 pairs of shoes, twp 6-foot boards that are about 2 inches wide, and glue or screws (anything that secures the shoes to the board)

How much time does it take? 10 minutes (10 to 20 minutes of prep time)

Description: Lay the two boards parallel to one another. Attach the shoes (at least two pairs) to the boards. One shoe is on the left board and the other is on the right. Make sure the shoes are facing the same way.

The leader should clear a path for the team to walk from one end of the room to the other wearing the shoes. If there are more team members than there are shoes you may need to repeat the exercise.

Discuss how the team members felt about working together. How did they accomplish the task? Did they feel that others were working against their efforts? Did it take everyone working together to accomplish the task?

105. **Big Foot Alternate Version**

Description: This version is much more difficult. Blindfold the "walkers" and have the other team members coach them across the room. They cannot touch the team members; they can only guide them verbally. For a greater challenge, you can have the group walk backwards.

106. **Champagne**

Purpose: Problem solving, creativity

Group size: 2+

Level: Basic

What do you need? Dish soap, straws, and string

How much time does it take? 15+ minutes

Description: The team has to create bubbles using the supplies given to them. Break the team up into small groups and see who can create the largest bubble.

How did it feel to create something with nontraditional tools? What was the process to accomplish the goal? Did everyone participate?

107. Champagne Advanced Version

Description: In this version, the leader gives the team very diluted soap. The leader should put the soap where the team can easily access it. The group will need to add more soap in order to make bubbles, but must be creative and motivated to add the soap.

Did the team give up without trying to fix the soap? Did they work as a team to figure out the problem? Did they ask permission to use the soap or did they just use it? Did the group get frustrated?

108. The Bait and Switch Hunt

Purpose: Teamwork, competition

Group Size: 6+ (at least two groups)

Level: Basic

What do you need? Pencils for each group, paper for each group

How much time does it take? 45+ minutes

Description: Each team creates a scavenger hunt list. The rule is that they must be able to find the item themselves. Each team should make a list of at least ten items. The leader then switches the lists. The leader should give a time limit to find the items and bring them back (or take a picture of the item). The team that finds the most items wins.

Did one group try to sabotage another? How did it feel to create a list that was fair for your team members? Did you set them up to fail? How did the team search for the items? Did team members hide the items to make it harder for their competition to find?

109. Badminton by the Numbers

Purpose: Teamwork

Group Size: 6+

Level: Basic

What do you need? Badminton set and a die

How much time does it take? 30+ minutes (20 minutes of prep time)

Description: The game of badminton is played under normal rules except that before a team serves the bird, the leader roles a dice. The rolled number is the amount of times the team has to hit the bird before they serve it over the net or the other team gets the point.

How hard was this to do? Was it harder than regular badminton? Did it take extra teamwork and communication to accomplish? Did it utilize more team members than a normal game would? How did everyone feel about being included in the game?

110. Team Body Art

Purpose: Teamwork and creativity

Group Size: 4+

Level: Basic

What do you need? No extra items are needed

How much time does it take? 10+ minutes

Description: The team is challenged to become a certain work of art by using only their bodies. Everyone in the group must be a part of the work of art. The leader may set time limits for the team to create the artwork.

How did it feel to be a part of the team in this exercise? Was it hard to include everyone? Did everyone have a part in deciding how to create the artwork?

Here is a list of possible art pieces.

- Octopus
- A ca
- A windmill
- An orchestra
- A football field
- Christmas Day

- A spider
- A truck
- A waterwheel
- A clock
- A rock concert
- Halloween party

111. Team Body Art Advanced

Description: The game is played the same as the first except that the team is broken into two or more groups. The first team is given an object, but the other teams do not know what it is. They have a certain amount of time to make a work of art and the other teams must guess what it is. Teams are awarded points for correct guesses. The team that had the most art pieces identified correctly wins. This may confuse the team members if they think that the guesses were more important than the creations.

How was it different to have another team guess what the object or scene was? Was it harder to do? Did the team change around to make it easier for the other team to guess or did they work against the other team to win the game?

112. **Disk Badminton**

Purpose: Teamwork and cooperation

Group Size: 6+ (enough to make two teams)

Level: Basic

What do you need? Badminton Set and enough Frisbees for each team member plus two extra for each side

Example: 6 players + 4 extra Frisbees = 10 Frisbees

How much time does it take? 20+ minutes (20+ minutes of prep time)

Description: The leader spreads out the Frisbees equally on each side of the net. The teams must start with everyone standing on a Frisbee. During the game, everyone must be on a Frisbee and only one person can be on a Frisbee at a time. Team members can go to an empty Frisbee during the game. The regular badminton rules apply.

Did this take teamwork to accomplish? Did anyone argue over a Frisbee? Did everyone have a chance to play the game? Did some players try to dominate? Did this hurt the game?

113. **Chocolate Gold Rush**

Purpose: Teamwork

Group Size: 6+ (in pairs)

Level: Basic

What do you need? Wrapped chocolates. If someone on the team cannot eat chocolate, make sure you include treats that they can eat. You also need a carpet scrap big enough for two people to stand on but not much larger. If no carpet is available, the leader can tape off a small area.

How much time does it take? 20+ minutes

Description: The carpet is put in the center of the room. The goodies are placed all around the scrap, just far enough that it would be difficult for one person to reach. The team is broken up into pairs.

The rules are as follows:

- No body part may touch outside the carpet at anytime or you lose your turn

- No object may be used to pull the chocolate toward the pair

- The chocolate must be picked up, not slid, or dragged

- There is a time limit

The way to do this task is for one of the pair to hold the other while he or she grabs the chocolate. This should not be told until after the exercise. You may need to add candy, as some pairs will be better than others.

How did they figure out the activity? How did it feel to rely on someone to hold you up to achieve a goal?

114. **Frankenstein's Monster**

Purpose: Teamwork

Group Size: 6+

Level: Basic

What do you need? A large piece of butcher paper and a pen

How much time does it take? 15+ minutes

Description: The task is to act like Doctor Frankenstein. The team creates a figure with one body part from each member. Each team member must lie on the paper and have one body part traced as part of the team monster. The team can color in and decorate the monster.

What was the end result? How did it feel to be a part of a larger entity? How did your body part fit on the creature? Who decided what body part people were going to use? Was there a vision of what the creature looked like before they started?

115. **One, Double, Triple**

Purpose: Teamwork

Group Size: 6+ (at least two teams)

Level: Basic

What do you need? Pick a team sport such as badminton, soccer, or basketball, and an area to play the game

How much time does it take? 20+ minutes

Description: The game is played the normal way, except that the scoring is different. For each team member the scoring is as follows:

1st score = 6 points

2nd score = 2 points

3rd score and beyond = 1 point each

The goal is to have each team member score at least once because the score will be higher than if one member scores all the time.

How did it feel to be included in scoring for the team? Did team members help another member score for the extra points? Did this encourage more teamwork?

116. **Over, Under and Through the Woods**

Purpose: Team abilities

Group Size: 4+

Level: Basic

What do you need? 2 ropes and 2 poles or trees at least 10 feet from one another

How much time does it take? 15+ minutes (5 minutes of prep time)

Description: The leader must tie the two ropes parallel to one another between the poles or trees. The top rope must be high enough to make it a struggle to get over but so that at least one team member will be tall enough to make it over without touching the ropes. The two ropes must be far enough apart so one team member can slip between them and the bottom rope should be high enough for someone to squeeze under without touching.

The task is for the group to get to grandmother's house on the other side of the electric fence. At least one team member must go over, one must go under, and one must go through the ropes. The other team members may duplicate any of these. If one person touches the rope and is "shocked," the team must start over until everyone can get to grandmother's house safely.

How did people's individual skills play into this exercise? Was the team able to complete the task? How many tries did it take? Did people have to try different ways until they could get through the fence? Was this frustrating for other people in the group? Did someone have to change the way they went because someone else could not make it?

117. I Scream, You Scream, We All Scream for Ice Cream

Purpose: Teamwork, team initiative

Group Size: 4+

Level: Advanced

What do you need? Ice cream maker, rock salt, ingredients to make homemade ice cream, a recipe card, bowls, spoons, ice

How much time does it take? 30+ minutes

Description: Place all the items around the room and put one empty bowl and spoon in front of you. This is a good exercise to do at the end of the day or after lunch. Say nothing except "Go." Look at the bowl and at your watch and say nothing further. The goal is to see if the team has enough initiative to make ice cream without being told. They have been given the tools and the permission.

If they do not understand at first, you can give them subtle hints. Look into the bowl and then at your watch. Lick your lips a couple of times. Rub your stomach, but do not say anything.

After they make the ice cream ask them some questions. Who decided to initiate a move and start making the ice cream? Who ran the project? Was everyone involved? How long did it take them to figure out the task? Were they scared to make a move without instructions? What finally sent the message about what the task was? Do they always need to be told what to do or do they have group initiative and leadership?

118. Resource Utilization Version 1

Purpose: Resource utilization

Group Size: 6+ (2 or more teams)

Level: Basic

What do you need? Resources such as phone books, pamphlets, newsletters, magazines, or newspapers

How much time does it take? 15+ minutes

Description: The resources are piled in the middle of the room. Each team can send one team member at a time to run and grab a resource. Once the resource is used, it must be returned before another can be used.

The leader shouts out a particular resource and the teams must try to find it before the other team does.

Here is a list of possible resources

- Police
- Italian restaurant
- List of local dentists
- Building supplies
- Newspaper wanted ads

The leader may pick resources that team members need to be able to access for their jobs. The team with the most finds wins.

119. **Resource Utilization Version 2**

Purpose: Resource utilization

Group Size: 6+ (2 or more teams)

Level: Basic

What do you need? Computers. This will only work if there are least two computers that the groups can use

How much time does it take? 15+ minutes

Description: The groups must find the resources on the Internet. Group members must take turns working the computer. Once a round is complete, another team member sits down. Team members can help by telling the computer operator where to go on the Internet.

How did it feel to have others telling you what to do? Could you do the task on your own? Did the team slow you down?

120. J Is for Jumping Jacks

Purpose: Getting to know your team

Group Size: 4+

Level: Basic

What do you need? Paper and pens

How much time does it take? 20+ minutes

Description: Each team member will break down his or her name by letter. Each letter will represent a word and each word will mean something about that team member. Here is an example for John:

Junior: My father is John Senior

Orchestra: I play the piccolo in an orchestra

Hiking: Hiking is one of my favorite pasttimes

Never: I am always late and never on time for appointments

After they create their names, they must share them with their partners. They can introduce themselves to other members of the group.

Was it easier to learn and remember a person's name this way? Were some of the examples clever? Did you learn new things about your team members?

121. J Is for Jumping Jacks Alternate Version

Description: In this version, people are paired together. They must share their names with their partners. Then the partners introduce one another to the group, using the words to help them remember their team member's names.

122. Quarter of a Century

Purpose: Getting to know your team

Group Size: 6+

Level: Basic

What do you need? A different quarter for each person

How much time does it take? 15+ minutes

Description: Each person takes a different quarter (you can have fun if you find at least one really old quarter). Have the team members introduce themselves to the rest of the team. They must include something exciting that happened to them or is somehow related to them on the year that is on the quarter.

Did they learn something new about their team members?

123. Better Than That

Purpose: Getting to know your team

Group Size: 4+

Level: Basic

What do you need? Nothing extra is needed

How much time does it take? 15+ minutes

Description: In this exercise, the leader starts by talking about something he or she enjoys doing. The next person must say that what they like to do is better and state what it is. This continues to go around the team until the leader stops the exercise or someone gets stumped.

Here is an example:

"I like to eat pizza."

"I like something better than that. I like to watch old movies."

Did they learn something new about their team members?

124. **Common Ground**

Purpose: Getting to know your team

Group Size: 6+

Level: Basic

What do you need? Paper and pens

How much time does it take? 15+ minutes

Description: The group must introduce themselves to other people on the team and make two columns on their paper. The first column contains things they have in common with each other and second contains a piece of information that they do not have in common. The person with the most names during a time limit wins.

What do the team members have in common with one another? Were there interesting differences?

125. **Crazy Eights**

Purpose: Problem solving

Group Size: 6+

Level: Advanced

What do you need? Bean bag and a stopwatch

How much time does it take? 20+ minutes

Description: Have the team sit or stand in a circle. Hand the bag to any member and then explain the rules. The first person must throw the bean bag to someone else in the circle. The bean bag cannot go to any person twice. When everyone has had a turn the last person throws the bean bag to the first. Tell the team that they must memorize whom they threw the bag to.

Have the team repeat the design they made, and use the watch to see how fast they can do it. Repeat this a couple of times. Get the team to create a strategy to throw faster. Then time them again.

Was it important for every team member to work together? Was there a strategy to get the ball to move faster?

126. Crazy Eights Alternate Version

Description: In this version, add a bag to weave through the pattern. You can keep adding bean bags to see if they can keep the pattern moving. If they drop the bag, they must start over with one bag. The purpose is not speed, but rather coordination and paying attention.

Was it more difficult to keep the pattern going with more bags?

127. Pass the Cup

Purpose: Coordination and strategy

Group Size: 8+ (2 or more teams)

Level: Basic

What do you need? A stack of paper or plastic cups (30 per team)

How much time does it take? 10+ minutes (5 minutes of prep time)

Description: Make two rows of chairs. Place each stack of cups on one end of each row. Have the team members sit in the chairs. The task is to get the cups from one end of the row to the other. The cups must be passed from the person's left hand to their right hand and then passed from their right hand to the next person's left hand. Each person must participate and no one can get up from his or her chair.

128. Pass the Cup Alternate Version

Description: In this version, every other person is blindfolded. They have to rely on cues from the people on each side of them. They can communicate by any technique other than touch.

How did it feel to be reliant on others? What techniques were used to solve this problem?

129. Team Geometry

Purpose: Teamwork

Group Size: 5+

Level: Advanced

What do you need? 50 to 100 feet of rope

How much time does it take? 15+ minutes

Description: All team members must grab a part of the rope. No one may switch places with anyone else. The team must form the shape of the number 8 with the rope and with no rope left over.

How did the team figure this task out? Did everyone have to cooperate? Did everyone communicate?

130. Team Geometry Alternate Version #1

Description: In this version, other shapes are created. Some are much harder than others. Here is a list of sample shapes:

- Triangle
- Square
- Star
- The team logo
- A name
- Other numbers

131. Team Geometry Alternate Version #2

Description: In this version, the team is split up into two groups. They must form the shape using both ropes. No group member may grab a different rope.

Was it harder to coordinate two groups in a single task? What were the challenges?

132. Can You Count?

Purpose: Problem solving

Group Size: 8+

Level: Advanced

What do you need? A deck of cards and three sheets of paper

How much time does it take? 20+ minutes

Description: Each team member is assigned a playing card. The card can be of any suit, ace through eight (more or less depending on the size of the group). Place the sheets of paper in front of the team. They can only touch their card during the game. Have the team stack the cards from 8 to ace, with the ace on top. These are stacked on one sheet of paper.

The team must restack the cards in the same order on another sheet of paper. Here are the rules:

- Only one card can be moved at a time.

- The cards can be placed on any sheet of paper.

- A higher number card cannot be placed onto a lower number card. For example: 4 can not be placed onto a 3, 2, or ace. However, a 4 can be placed onto a 5, 6, 7 or 8.

Was this task difficult? Was it harder because everyone had to be responsible for his or her own card? What strategy did the team come up with?

133. **What Do You Think?**

Purpose: Problem solving

Group Size: 4+

Level: Advanced

What do you need? Paper and pens

How much time does it take? 20+ minutes

Description: Each team member must write one problem that they are facing at work or in being a part of the team.

When everyone has written his or her problem, the group passes the paper to the person on the right. The next person takes a few moments and writes a possible solution under the problem. The papers are shifted from person to person, until everyone has commented on every problem.

Was this helpful? Did you find solutions you had not thought of? Will any of the solutions work?

134. **New Software**

Purpose: Problem solving

Group Size: 4+

Level: Advanced

What do you need? No extra materials are needed

How much time does it take? 45+ minutes

Description: The leader says that the team was given new software. The software is supposed to be better than the old software and make their lives easier. Upon using the software, the team realizes that not only does it not do what was promised, but also that the software is full of bugs that often crash the system. The team tried to explain the problem to management. Management states that the software is fine and cost the company a lot of money. If production falls behind, management will want to know why and would then reconsider their position.

What does the team do? Are there ethical questions concerning this practice? How is the final decision made? Was it voted on?

135. The Volcano Is Ready to Blow

Purpose: Decision making

Group Size: 6+

Level: Advanced

What do you need? Paper and pens

How much time does it take? 45+ minutes (10 minutes of prep time)

Description: The leader tells the team that they are on an island for vacation. A volcano is about to blow and they must get off the island. The boat has been damaged and currently does not work.

Give the team different options of what they should do. Here are some suggestions:

- Fix the boat • Call for help   • Signal a plane
- Send a few people for help on a small life raft

Each team member ranks the ideas from 1 to 15. Then, as a group, they must rank the ideas from 1 to 15. 1 is the best idea, and 15 is the worst idea.

Compare how the individual rankings differ from the group's rankings. How did they decide to rank as a group? Was it a fair process? Was everyone included? Were everyone's rankings about the same?

136. **The Volcano Is Ready to Blow Advanced Version**

Description: In this version, a third set of rankings is added. This is a volcano expert's ranking (you are the expert and should do this ahead of time). Have the team compare these rankings with their own. Give them a chance to change either the group rankings or the individual rankings.

Did people change their answers? Why? Were they swayed by how other people said it should be done? Why?

137. **Said the Spider to the Fly**

Purpose: Teamwork

Group Size: 6+

Level: Advanced

What do you need? String. This needs to be done outdoors between two trees or poles.

How much time does it take? 20+ minutes (20+ minutes of prep time)

Description: The leader must create a web using the string. The web is tied between the two trees or poles. The holes in the web must be big enough to allow team members to crawl through without touching any string. These holes can be various sizes to add to the challenge.

The task is to get team members through the web without touching a string. Once a person makes it through a hole, the group cannot use that hole again. Everyone must make it to the other side. If someone touches a string, the whole team must start over. They can crawl between the ground and the web one time, as that counts as a hole. The web cannot be altered in any way.

How did the team work out a strategy? Was everyone important in completing this task?

138. Said the Spider to the Fly Alternate Version

Description: In this version, the team is split into two groups. This is more competitive. Each team takes turns and the rules are the same. Whenever anyone from either team goes through a hole, it is closed. The team that can get all of their members through first, wins.

Was this harder? Was there greater strategy involved? Did the group work on a strategy together to complete the task?

139. Piranha

Purpose: Teamwork

Group Size: 5+

Level: Advanced

What do you need? Frisbees, tape

How much time does it take? 20+ minutes

Description: The leader marks off a 25-foot wide river. One Frisbee will be given for every two people. The water is full of man-eating fish. If any part of a person's body touches the water, the fish will eat it. On the other side of the river is a phone. Everyone must make it to that side of the river to call for help and make it back across the river to wait for help.

If any part of anyone's body touches the water, the game must be restarted. The Frisbees are magical floating river stones. If someone's foot is not touching the stone, the fish will eat it.

During the course of play, the leader will take a stone if at least one person is not touching it. You cannot slide the stones at anytime.

Was this a difficult activity? What process was used to solve the task? Was everyone able to make it back to safety?

140. **Rings**

Purpose: Ice breaker

Group Size: 4+ (in pairs)

Level: 1st

What do you need? No extra materials are needed

How much time does it take? 10+ minutes

Description: Have everyone find a partner. One partner is "one" and the other is "two." The "ones" are the inner circle and face outward. The "twos" are the outer circle. They pair up with their partner and face inward. The inner circle asks a question of the outer. The outer circle partners have one minute to answer. The leader says shift and the out circle moves one person to the left. The same question or a different question can be asked. The same time limit is applied. When everyone in the inner circle has asked everyone in the outer circle a question, it is the outward circle's turn to ask questions. The questions can be about anything, or the leader may state that it needs to be work related.

Was this an easy way to meet and get to know people? Was it awkward? Did you wish you had more time with particular people?

141. **Cow Fence**

Purpose: Teamwork

Group Size: 4+

Level: Basic

What do you need? A rope, 2 poles or trees

How much time does it take? 10+ minutes

Description: The leader must tie the rope between the trees or poles just below waist height. This is a cow fence and cannot be touched or will sound an alarm. The team is a herd of cows making a break for freedom. They cannot touch the line in anyway and must get over the line together. Everyone in the herd should be touching the herd at all times. The herd must go over the line, not under or around. If the rules are broken the team must start over.

Did everyone work together? How many tries did it take? What was the strategy?

142. Mouse in the Pipe

Purpose: Teamwork

Group Size: 4+

Level: Basic

What do you need? 1 marble, a small length of pipe for each team member, a cup

How much time does it take? 20+ minutes

Description: Place the cup on the opposite side of the room from the team. The task is to get the marble to the cup by using only the pipes. They cannot touch the marble and the marble cannot fall or they have to start over again. They cannot move while the marble is in their pipe. Once the marble leaves their pipe they can walk again.

Was this activity hard? Did it take everyone's help? Did everyone participate?

143. Mouse in the Pipe Advanced Version

Purpose: Teamwork

Description: In this version, a cup is set on each side of the room. Each marble starts on one side of the room and must go across the room to the cup. The marbles cannot be in the same pipe at the same time. This is much harder to accomplish.

What was the strategy for this one? Did the team split in two? Did everyone try to work with both marbles at once?

144. Storm Is Coming

Purpose: Teamwork

Group Size: 6+

Level: Advanced

What do you need? Old newspapers, masking tape

How much time does it take? 50+ minutes

Description: The team is told that a hurricane is coming. They must build a shelter using the paper and tape to cover everyone before it hits. They have 25 minutes to plan and 25 minutes to build the shelter. No one can speak while they are building.

Was the team able to build it? What was the strategy? How did the team communicate while building? Was preplanning important?

144. Numbers

Purpose: Problem solving

Group Size: 4+

Level: Basic

What do you need? Paper, pens, and a stopwatch

How much time does it take? 30+ minutes (10+ minutes prep time)

Description: The leader must write a number on each piece of paper and set the numbers on the floor in this pattern:

10 26 34 2　　9　25 33 1

46 42 38 18 45 41 37 17

14 30 22 6　　13 29 21 5

12 28 36 4　　11 27 35 3

48 44 40 20 47 43 39 19

16 32 24 8　　15 31 23 7

The object is for team members to touch the numbers in order. Have a couple of them try it. While the numbers may seem random, they are actually in a grid of 4 boxes of 12.

2　　　　　1

4　　　　　3

All the numbers fall within that grid. If the team can figure this out they can do it much faster. Another solution is to move the numbers into an easier order. Tell the team that for every number they touch out of turn, they must start over.

Did the team work together? Did they come up with a strategy? Did people help one another? Did people compete with one another?

145. Factory Line

Purpose: Teamwork

Group Size: 6+ (2 or more groups)

Level: Basic

What do you need? Bean bags

How much time does it take? 15+ minutes

Description: Have the groups get into circles. Each person must be far enough away from the other that they have to toss, rather than hand, the beanbag to each other.

Have the teams toss the bag around one time. Each person must touch it once, but only one team member can touch it at a time. The bag cannot touch the floor or the team has to start over. Once they understand the concept, have the groups try to speed up the process. Time them to see which team can do it the fastest.

Was there a strategy to making it go faster? Did repeating the exercise make the groups more efficient in completing the task?

146. Factory Line Advanced Version

Description: In this exercise, the leader will change the rules as the team progresses.

- Remove a team member and tell the group that someone called in sick

- Remove another team member and tell the group that someone went on vacation

- Add a bag and tell the group that management wants to double output

- Have someone only use one hand, because they were injured on the job

- Have a few group members leave, because the team went on strike

- Change group members and tell the group that they have new employees

How did it feel to have changes occur? Did it slow production down? Was it frustrating? How did it feel to be removed from the group and have them pick up your load?

147. **Move the Hoop**

Purpose: Teamwork

Group Size: 6+

Level: Basic

What do you need? A hula hoop

How much time does it take? 10+ minutes

Description: The team stands in a line and holds hands. The leader places the hoop on the first person's arm. The task is to get the hula hoop down the line and back again without letting go hands. You can split the team and have a competition to see who can do it faster. Was it hard to do? Did some people struggle to get it moving? Did the team encourage them?

148. **There Is No "I" in Team or Is There?**

Purpose: Creative thinking

Group Size: 6+ (2 teams)

Level: 1st/Basic

What do you need? 2 posters, pens

How much time does it take? 10+ minutes

Description: One team is given the word "team." The other group is given the word "self."

The group with the word "team" must create an acronym with the letters in the word. The words must represent qualities that a good team needs. The team with the word "self" must create an acronym of qualities that are avoided in a good team. They should write these on the posters, decorate them, and share them with the group.

How did it feel to use the word "self" in a negative way? Did this create an emotional response? Can "self" and "team" exist together?

149. I Would Like You to Meet

Purpose: Ice breaker

Group Size: 6+

Level: 1st

What do you need? Paper, markers, and tape

How much time does it take? 10+ minutes

Description: Have each person write his or her name on the piece of paper. Tape the paper to the back of the person and have the team mingle with one another for a few minutes. They are to write a word that describes their first impression on the back of the appropriate person. When everyone is finished, the leader has people read each other's backs. They are to introduce the person using the words that were written.

How did the words people used about you make you feel? Were these fair? Are first impressions important?

150. Characteristics Bingo

Purpose: Ice breaker

Group Size: 10+

Level: 1st/Basic

What do you need? Paper and pens

How much time does it take? 15 minutes (15 minutes of prep time)

Description: Create a bingo board that is 5 by 5 squares. Put information in the squares that would apply to people on the team. Here are examples:

- Has more than two children

- Has been with the company more than three years

- Owns a red car

Be creative. The better the leader knows the team members the more creative he or she can be. Copy the boards and give them out to the team. Have them ask questions of each other. If the person they are talking to relates to a square, have them initial it. The person that has the first initials across, diagonal, or down wins. Each person can only initial one space.

Did you learn new things about your team members?

4

Communication Activities

Communication is essential for a team to work together. Without it, many team members will feel lost and alone. Communication has to begin from the top and continue strong all the way down the ladder of directors, supervisors, and workers.

I would suggest that supervisors be given the time and tools to have mini team events, like brainstorming sessions on how to improve productivity once or twice a month, finding ways to recognize team achievements in friendly competition with other groups of employees at the worksite or organization, or hosting a monthly interactive discussion about important topics like harassment and quality. Serving a free pizza lunch as a reward for exceeding production targets on an occasional basis works well to build morale, but be careful. If free food and free gifts are given without being tied to specific goals, employees will see them as entitlements and not rewards.

In some areas of our plant in St. Louis, managers have taken a top-down approach, barging in and changing a bunch of things, without properly communicating, without gaining input of the employees, and without involving the supervisors in the process. In these areas, there has been resistance to the changes, a larger number of grievances from the union employees, and a higher number of employees leaving, some even taking lower paying jobs in other areas.

Stephen Coenen

The following activities are designed to help your team communicate with each other more effectively. Communication is not always verbal. Sometimes people communicate with body language, gestures, or even a light touch. These activities incorporate all types of communication.

In addition to communicating with others, team members have to learn how to give and accept feedback. This can be very difficult for some, and they may become defensive. These activities are fun, nonthreatening ways to break through these types of barriers. They are designed to teach team members how to give feedback respectfully with the intention of improving the team and that particular team member's performance. Feedback is not meant to hurt others or impose power and control over others.

Being able to give and accept positive feedback can be difficult for team members. They may not be comfortable with others telling them that they did a great job. Supervisors may find it difficult to recognize and point out things that a team is doing right because they are accustomed to pointing out the negative things.

When people become defensive, a few different things can occur. A team member may retreat and stop interacting with other team members if feedback is given or received inappropriately. In some work situations, like a hospital emergency room, this can bring the whole team to a screeching halt because, if one member is not interacting, other members cannot successfully perform their jobs. In a factory setting, if one person does not communicate with others down the line, work can stop and people could get hurt.

Communication is essential in a group that works together. I do exercises with my dance students that help them break down barriers between one another. They must be able to work together by being physically close and at times touching one another. This is a hard concept. I have them learn eye contact and nonverbal communication using their body. This is important when people are moving quickly past one another or having to hold each other up. Without this communication someone can get hurt. One of the first exercises I use is allowing the students to get close and yell at one another. This breaks down barriers and allows them to move past conventional standards and allows them to communicate at a deeper and more meaningful level.

Retreating from others when threatened is a natural instinct. It is called the fight or flight response. Our ancestors, when faced with a large animal, had two choices. Either they ran away or they took a spear and tried to fight the animal. While we do not have to worry about saber-toothed tigers anymore, our natural instinct for survival still remains. When we are cornered or feel anxious, our body prepares itself for running or fighting. Hormones are released and blood is pumped harder to our extremities. Since fighting in a work place will probably get most people fired, they usually respond by fleeing. When they cannot physically flee then they flee mentally and emotionally. They become cold and irritable. They do not interact and their ability to communicate is greatly reduced.

That is why being able to practice and receive feedback is important. You should become accustomed to receiving feedback, knowing that it is meant to help, not hurt. Learning how to give this feedback without being offensive or rude is a skill worth acquiring. It builds trust among team members and installs a mechanism for improvement when improvement is needed to accomplish a task.

You can take a whole teambuilding session or sessions and dedicate them to communication and feedback. Through these exercises, you may discover people have different communication styles. Recognizing this can be a very powerful tool. Some people can be used in certain situations just based on their style of communication.

Suppose that you have a worker that just had a pet pass away. They come to work and are visibly upset but will not talk to anyone about it. This affects the whole team because others are distracted by that team member's mood and that team member may not be doing their job efficiently that day. Having a confrontational or aggressive person talk to them may not be the ideal situation. Someone that is calm, soothing, and nurturing may be the best person to handle it.

On the other hand, if your company is having difficulty with a client and that client tries to intimidate others, sending someone who is quiet and meek may not be the best choice.

In addition to recognizing communication styles, being able to change those styles may be a larger task. Sometimes certain personalities and ways people communicate do not work well with certain types of teams. Helping the team and team member come up with a compromise and changing some of their behaviors can help reduce turnover and help make the team stronger and more efficient.

One of the main exercises I do to teach communication skills is role-playing activities. The team can learn both by playing the role and by observing the interaction. The exercises need to be short enough not to intimidate team members but long enough for them to truly think through situations before they act. Communication exercises can help solve many situations that may have existed for many years between team members. It is all about developing trust among team members."

Dan Comer

1. The Factory Machine

Purpose: Improve communication

Group Size: 8+ (broken into two teams)

Level: Advanced

What do you need? 2 bags and 10 bean bags or similar objects. They must be 2 different colors, or 5 of each color. You also need pieces of paper to be used as a pathway stones and 2 adjoining rooms or areas to work in. There must be a door separating the 2 rooms or areas.

How much time does it take? 20+ minutes (15 + minutes of prep time)

Description: The team is broken up into two groups. In each room or area, the leader must set up the playing area the same. At the far side of the room, away from the door, a bag with 5 same colored bean bags is set up. The pieces of paper are used as pathways from the door to the bag. Each piece of paper is placed a couple of feet from the next.

Have the groups go to their rooms and close the door in between. Tell each group that they must get rid of their beanbags from the room and they must gather the beanbags from the other room and put them in their bag. They must stay on the pathway stones at all times. No beanbags can cross each other's path. The group members may not leave their room. Once a beanbag has begun to move forward, it cannot move back. If any of the rules are violated, the exercise must start over.

The groups must communicate to complete this exercise. Discuss with the team how they were able to work out the exercise. How did they communicate? Was communication before attempting the exercise important? Is it important for teams to be able to work with other teams in order to be able to complete tasks? How has this worked in the past? Is communication important to get tasks completed between teams? Is it hard to communicate on a project when the two teams are in different places? How did not being able to see what the other group was doing affect their team to be able to complete the task?

2. **White Water Rafting**

   Purpose: Communication

   Group Size: 4+

   Level: Advanced

   What do you need? Blindfold, obstacles (rocks), cookie for each river guide

How much time does it take? 10+ minutes (10+ minutes of prep time)

Description: Set up a river with obstacles that the river raft must avoid or it will crash. The team is blindfolded and the river guides set themselves near the rocks. The guides must navigate the boat by verbal commands around the rocks. If the team gets past the rocks, they deliver a cookie (passenger) to the river guide. They then make their way to the next guide. Each guide can only give directions when the boat is in his or her part of the river. If the boat crashes, the team does not get the cookie and the boat continues to the next guide. The guides can give words of encouragement when the boat is in another part of the river, just not directions. And yes, the team can eat the cookies when they are finished (even the guides who crashed the boat). Switch the members to be different guides and river boats.

Discuss how it felt to be a boat and how it felt to be a river guide. How did it feel to watch another river guide direct the boat and not be able to help? How did it feel to get the cookie (reinforcement)? How did it feel to see the boat crash and not get a cookie?

3. White Water Rafting Alternate Version

Description: In addition to cookies, have passengers on the boat also be blindfolded. They can place their hand on the person's shoulder in front of them. At each successful navigation, a person can get off the boat. How did this feel to be a passenger? Did this change how the boat felt to be responsible for passengers?

4. Special Report

Purpose: Communication

Group Size: 6+ (two teams)

Level: Advanced

What do you need? Paper, pen

How much time does it take? 60+ minutes

Description: The team is split into two groups. Each must present a radio or TV special report about the other team. It should be about 15 minutes in length. They can include music, a weather report, or anything else that works in the special report. The report has to include every member of the other team. Here are some ideas for the report:

- Meteor crashes in small town

- Flood covers an island

- Family won the lottery

- Team awarded an international prize

- Lunchtime yesterday

- Teambuilding exercises change team forever

- First team in space

The purpose is to include everyone on the other team and have updates about how they are doing and what role they played in the report. After they create the broadcast they should share it with the other group.

Was it difficult to include everyone in the report? Did everyone on the team participate? How did the team members communicate during this exercise? Did everyone feel they were heard?

5. Special Report Alternate Version

Description: In this version, everyone on the team had a reporting role. They can be on the scene, in the studio, or on the phone with the other broadcasters. This will take extra time. They can have props, music, and sound effects.

How did it feel to work with others to create the report? Was your role important? How did each team member hand off the next part of the report to another reporter or broadcaster? Was there clear communication about who was doing what?

6. **Blind Man's Tag**

   Purpose: Communication

   Group Size: 4 + (divided into pairs)

   Level: Advanced

   What do you need? Blindfolds, open area to play

   How much time does it take? 10 to 20 minutes

   Description: One person in each pair will be blindfolded. Explain to the team that they need to play in a certain area. You can mark this off with chairs or other articles if you wish. Choose one of the pairs as the pair to be "it." They are the ones that will try to tag the other blindfolded people. The sighted people in the pairs try to get their blindfolded partners away from the "it" person. The sighted "it" partner tries to direct his partner to tag the others. If they are tagged, they become the "it" person. The sighted partners can only use voice commands to tell their blindfolded partners where to go. Halfway into the game, have the partners switch positions. Afterward, talk about how it felt to be the sighted one and then being blindfolded. Use it as a tool to discuss communication and trust issues among the team members.

It is a good idea to close with a lessons learned discussion. Have everyone involved share at least one comment, such as what is one thing new you noticed today about the group. A small survey, or a way to give anonymous feedback, is very important. This allows you to refine the exercise for later use or know where you need to take the group next. Another option to consider is forming a small group of participants who you can bounce future ideas off of so that you are not working in the dark. This also allows the participants to feel ownership in the process.

Long term, if the group continues to work together, monitor their progress. Make notes of when morale is low and inject new life into the group with another day or half day of fun exercises. Periodically, all groups should step back and do teambuilding exercises just to keep things fresh. Your group may need something once a month, or only once a year.

Michelle Lovejoy

I have facilitated a discussion-oriented harassment training at my current job at Covidien to groups of employees. The training involved group discussion, followed by each group presenting how they perceive certain stereotypes of women, gay people, etc. from the past compared to the present time. In my experience, adults learn better when they have a chance to discuss ideas with others as part of the training and have a chance to use the knowledge taught in some sort of activity or game.

Stephen Coenen

7. **Circle Seat**

Purpose: Communication

Group Size: 6+

Level: Advanced

What do you need? Space to make a circle

How much time does it take? 5 minutes for activity, 10 to 20 minutes for discussion

Description: Have everyone stand shoulder to shoulder, facing toward the center of the circle. Then, have everyone turn so that their right shoulder is inside the circle, their left is outside, and they are facing the back of the person who was to their left. Have the group take a step or two toward the center so that the circle is tighter. Then, on the count of three, everyone sits down on the lap of the person behind them. Lead a conversation about physical contact and why it feels uncomfortable to be close or not, bringing in cultural questions of space between two people.

Teambuilding provides an opportunity for groups of people to get to know each other very quickly. The participants have to work closely together, physically supporting each other in physical challenges and communicating ideas and words of encouragement. Personal barriers are quickly broken down, as the group must work together to accomplish the goal. The activities build on the strength of the team and not the individual. Activities can be done in convention centers, office buildings, city parks, etc. with little or no equipment. Where getting to know each other in a meeting environment may take weeks or months, the teambuilding activities build community and working toward the same goal in a matter of minutes or hours. The activities also highlight the creative problem solvers and identify natural public speakers and the extrovert leaders in the group. It is a chance to get to know each other outside the office cubical and e-mails.

The action of doing a teambuilding activity is important, but processing the experience afterward is the golden nugget that is taken away from the experience.

Processing is generating discussion on what happened during the activity, how they feel, learning from the situation, and setting goals for the future by transferring what they learned to real life and job situations.

Deb Dowling

---

8. Create a Design

Purpose: Communication

Group Size: 4+ divided into pairs

Level: Basic

What do you need? Legos or Tinker Toys. You need enough for each member of the team. You need to have the same pieces for each person. 10 or fewer pieces are suggested.

How much time does it take? 10 to 30 minutes (prep time of 10 minutes to sort Legos into piles for each team member)

Description: Partners sit with their backs to each other so they cannot see what the other is doing. Each person is given a set of identical Legos. Partner A creates a design on the table/floor and describes the design to Partner B. The first time this is done, Partner B cannot ask any questions of Partner A. The roles are reversed and the same thing is done. Then, the activity is repeated for each pair, and this time the person receiving the directions can ask questions.

9. **Dock Worker**

   Purpose: Communication

   Group Size: 4+

   Level: Basic

   What do you need? Rope or tape, objects for obstacles. Create a river using rope or tape on the floor with obstacles like people or chairs in the river.

   How much time does it take? 15+ minutes

   Description: One person is the dock worker, and he or she stands at one end of the river with another person who is blindfolded standing at the other end of the river. The dock worker gives directions for the other person to navigate the river without running into an obstacle.

10. **Zip Zap Zop**

Purpose: Communication

Group Size: 4+

Level: Basic

What do you need? No materials needed

How much time does it take? 15+ minutes

Description: Everyone in the group stands in a circle. One person is chosen to start the game and points to someone else in the circle and says, "zip." The second person points to a third person and says, "zap." The third person points to a fourth person and says "Zop." And then it starts over again with "zip." The goal is to get this going around the circle as fast as possible. If a person gets zipped, zapped, or zopped and does not immediately pass it on, they are out. Keep going until there is one person left.

11. **Hot Topic**

Purpose: Communication

Group Size: 4+

Level: Advanced

What do you need? Paper and pens

How much time does it take? 20 to 30 minutes (10 minutes of prep time)

Description: The leader should do some preparation and choose a topic that is current, applies to the team, and that may be controversial. The leader explains that the team is going to deal with the issue in a new way. Have the team members make a statement about the issue in a positive way instead of a negative way. Try to keep it simple and non-offensive.

For example: "People are taking extra time at lunch."

This can be rephrased as: "Being on time to work helps keep people on task and efficient."

Have the group scale their feelings about the "hot topic." The scale can be from 1 to 10. 1 would be very little feeling about it and 10 would be very upset. Have them write the number on a slip of paper and fold it. Have them put the slips of paper in a container. The leader mixes up the papers. This helps keep the team members anonymous. The leader then calculates the average score. The leader should keep this number to themselves at this point.

Ask the team members to predict what they think the average score is about the subject. Announce the average score and reward the team member that came the closest to the average number.

Break the team into 3 groups: 1s, 10s, and judges. The 1s and 10s should spend about 5 to 10 minutes coming up with an argument in support of their side. The 1s are not in support of changing the situation. The 10s are in support of creating some sort of change. Each team will have 5 minutes to argue their case to the judges. The judges write down the 2 sets of arguments. They review the 2 arguments and make a decision about the winner.

Note: This can go beyond a teambuilding game and be used as an actual team decision tool.

12. **Hot Topic Alternate Version**

   Description: In this version, you can make it like a courtroom drama. You can add props and make it very dramatic. Do not let it get too silly or the impact of the exercise could be lost.

13. **Buy It (Part 1)**

Purpose: Communication

Group Size: 6+ (at least two teams)

Level: Advanced

What do you need? A chalkboard or flipchart, pen or chalk to write on board, objects to be used for building, play money (each group gets $100 in alternate version), paper and pen for each team

How much time does it take? The first part will take 20+ minutes (10 to 15 minutes of prep time)

Description: This is part one of two exercises. They can be used together or as individual exercises.

Break the team into two smaller groups. On the board or flipchart write down the objects to be bought. The object of the exercise is to get the group from one side of a specified area to the other. The area should be at least 12 yards wide. The group must buy the materials in order to build the bridge that will get them across the space. They cannot touch the ground with their feet at any time.

Flip a coin to see which team goes first. Each team must bid on the objects presented. They can only spend their $100 on the objects. For example:

Team A	Team B
$10 on rope	$75 on paper
$40 on board	$25 on rope
$50 on paper	

The bidding is blind. Each team must write down their bids and turn them into the leader. The leader then distributes the objects to the teams based on their bids. Discuss with them if they think they can build the bridge based on what they bought. How did they work out the bids in their groups? What was their bridge design? Did they draw it out?

14. Buy It (Part 1) Alternate Version

Description: Instead of blind bidding, have them bid between each team like an auction. Have them use their play money to buy the objects.

Discuss how it felt to compete. How did they decide as a group what and how much to bid? Did they do it as a group or just let one member do the bidding?

15. Build It (Part 2)

Purpose: Communication

Cooperation: Creativity

Group Size: 6+ (at least 2 teams)

Level: Advanced

What do you need? Objects to be used for building, pen and paper for each team

How much time does it take? 20+ minutes (10+ minutes of prep time)

Description: If the group did Part 1, then they already have their objects to build a bridge. If they do not have the objects, then you can give each team the same objects to use.

The object of the exercise is for each group to build a bridge over an area that is at least 12 yards wide. The team must be able to cross it without touching the floor at anytime. Give them a time limit to accomplish the task. A successful team (or teams) can build the bridge and demonstrate how it works. Discuss how they felt about building the bridge. Did they draw it first? Did everyone participate? How did they feel about the process? Did they get competitive? How did that feel?

16. Build It (Part 2) Alternate Version #1

Description: Instead of assigning objects, tell each team that they have ten minutes to find three objects to build the bridge from around the room or building.

17. Build It (Part 2) Alternate Version #2

Description: Instead of a bridge, challenge the teams to build the tallest tower. You may want to add building blocks, pipe cleaners, or a set of Lincoln Logs (a toy that you can build a cabin out of sticks).

18. Blindman's Build

Purpose: Communication

Group Size: 4+ (at least two teams)

Level: Basic

What do you need? Blocks, blindfolds

How much time does it take? 15+ minutes (5 minutes of prep)

Description: The team is broken up into two groups, the sighted and the blind. The sighted group builds a simple structure using the blocks. The blind team looks and tries to memorize it. Then the blind team is blindfolded. The sighted team takes the blocks and places them around the room. The blindfolded must then find the pieces and rebuild the structure. The sighted team tells them where to go to get the pieces. They cannot touch the player or the block at any time. If it is taking a long time to complete, the leader may put a time limit on it. Once the team members find the pieces, the sighted members try to tell them how to build the structure. Switch the teams and repeat the activity.

Discuss with the team members how they completed the activity. How did they tell each member to find the pieces? Did they do them one by one? Did everyone participate?

19. **Team Black Jack**

    Purpose: Nonverbal communication

    Group Size: 9+ (in 3 or more teams)

    Level: Advanced

    What do you need? No materials needed

    How much time does it take? 10+ minutes

    Description: Break the team into at least three small groups. Like in the game blackjack, the goal is for the team to reach 21 using their fingers. They cannot communicate verbally with one another to accomplish this task.

    Have each group get into a circle facing one another and hold their hands behind their backs. The leader will say, "Ready, set, go."

    When the leader says, "go," the members are to hold out their hands in the middle of their circle. They are to hold zero to ten fingers each. The team that has 21 by counting all their fingers up wins. This may take a few turns before a group is able to do this. This is similar to the evens/odds game.

    Discuss with the group how they felt not being able to talk during the exercise. What kind of nonverbal communication did they use? How can a team accomplish a task without communicating clearly with each other?

20. **Hot Potato**

    Purpose: Communication

Group Size: 4+

Level: Advanced

What do you need? A ball or bean bag

How much time does it take? 10+ minutes

Description: Have the team sit in a circle. There are a few different ways you can do this activity. The object is to throw the ball or bean bag to another person in the circle and have that person say a specified thing and throw it to someone else. Here are some ideas:

- Have the group say the alphabet. Each person must say the next letter and throw the ball to someone else and they must say the next letter, and so on.

- This is the same as the ABC but the group must count. You can set the number of 100 as a goal.

- Find a simple play script and make copies for everyone. Assign each person a role in the script. After they finish their line, they must throw the ball to the next person who speaks.

- Find a poem and have each person say one word before they throw the ball to someone else.

- For a creative group, find the lyrics to a popular song. They must sing a word before passing it to someone else. The object is to actually have the group sing the song so the ball must be thrown fast.

- If the team is in charge of a particular process (like making a chair), have them break the process down and each team member must say what his or her role is and then throw the ball to the next person in the process. This can be a learning experience.

The rules are that if a person drops the potato, the group must start over until they can complete the activity. If a person says the wrong thing, then the group must start over.

Discuss how this activity made the group feel. Did they have to pay close attention? Did the other team members feel that another person was not pulling their load and messing the group up? How did they handle it? Were they excluded?

21. **The Talking Stick**

Purpose: Communication

Group Size: 4+

Level: Basic

What do you need? A stick

How much time does it take? 15 to 20 minutes

Description: The team gets into a circle. Only the person holding the talking stick can speak. The first person asks a question. He or she then passes the stick to the left and the person answers. Once the next person answers, he or she hands the stick to the person on his or her left. This continues until everyone has had a chance to answer. The next person then asks a question and the process is repeated. This process can go beyond the exercise and the talking stick can be used in all meetings – when a person holds the stick, everyone listens. When they want to say something, they raise their hand and wait for the stick. Here is a list of potential questions:

- If you could spend 24 hours with any person alive or dead, who would it be and why?

- Who is your favorite storybook character and why?

- What are the two events in your life that were the most significant and life altering?

- What are the three most important things in your life?

- What was the scariest thing that ever happened to you?

- What are your three favorite books and why?

- What are your three favorite foods and why?

- What are your three favorite movies and why?

- If you could have one wish, what would it be?

- If you were a superhero, who would you be?

Discuss your answers and how people felt. How did it feel to use the stick? Did you listen to others when they spoke or were you thinking about your answer only? Do you think the stick could work in other situations?

22. The Blind Line

Purpose: Communication, problem solving

Group Size: 4+

Level: Basic

What do you need? Blindfolds for everyone

How much time does it take? 10+ minutes

Description: Blindfold the team members and have them stand in a line. Have them rearrange themselves according to what parameters you give them. Here is a list of parameters that you could choose from:

- Shortest to tallest

- Oldest to youngest

- Longest with the company to the newest

- The team member with the largest family to the smallest family

- The largest car to the smallest car

Discuss how they solved getting in the line you described? Did someone take charge to get the others in line? Did team members feel vulnerable not being to see?

23. **The Blind Line Alternate Version #1**

   Description: This version is the same as the first except that the teams are given a time to complete each parameter.

   Discuss how team members felt about being under a deadline. Did it change how they solved the task? Did they cut corners? As a group leader you can give them the same amount of time it took them to solve the other tasks. After they complete it under a deadline, let them know that they had the same amount of time. Discuss how it felt being given the same amount of time but how it was different because of the deadline.

24. **The Blind Line Alternate Version #2**

   Description: This is the same as the first version except that a different team member is given the leader role and chooses a set of parameters.

   Discuss how it looked to the leader to see the team getting into the line. Have them compare differing perceptions of how well the group doe.

25. **The Big Picture**

   Purpose: Communication

   Group Size: 4+

   Level: Advanced

   What do you need? A large poster board or foamcore board, colored pens or pencils

How much time does it take? 20+ minutes (10 minutes of prep time)

Description: The leader cuts the board like large puzzle pieces so that each team member has his or her own piece. The goal is for the group to draw one large picture when the pieces are put back together. Allow 15 minutes to complete their pieces. When they are finished, put the puzzle together to see how the picture turned out.

Discuss why communication between team members was so important to complete the picture. How did they decide what to draw? Did one person direct the others? How did members feel about working with others to create something bigger? How did it feel to have their piece fit in with the others? Did it work?

26. The Big Picture Alternate Version

Description: In this version, do not allow the members of the team to see what the other team members are drawing. They can communicate with one another to try to complete the project verbally.

Discuss how this worked. Was it more difficult? Is it difficult to complete a project over the phone or Internet without seeing what the other person is doing?

27. What Comes Next?

Purpose: Listening skills

Group Size: 4+

Level: Basic

What do you need? A book of short stories

How much time does it take? 25+ minutes

Description: The leader should read a short story to the group. When the leader is finished, the group is given the task of naming at least one animal for every letter of the alphabet. When they have completed this task, begin the short story again. The leader should stop at different times and ask what comes next? The team member that can answer the question first wins a point. The leader continues to read and stop. The team member with the most points wins the game.

Was this a hard task for the team? Did anyone not remember any of the passages? Did something distract them?

28. **What Comes Next? Alternate Version #1**

Description: In this version, have a radio or some other sound that is distracting in the background while reading the story.

Did this make it harder for team members to remember?

29. **What Comes Next? Alternate Version #2**

Description: In this version, the team members must guess what the next line is. This is a much more difficult task and only people with very good memories can do this. Put the paper and pen in front of them, but do not tell them to use it or not use it.

Did anyone write down information when they were hearing it the first time? Did writing down information give anyone an advantage?

30. **Do You Hear What I Hear?**

Purpose: Listening skills

Group Size: 2+

Level: Basic

What do you need? Pen and paper

How much time does it take? 20+ minutes

Description: Have the team members write down noises they hear in the room. Give them a couple of minutes. Visit each area in which they work. Have them continue to write down sounds they hear. When you have completed the rounds, have the team members compare their lists.

Were team members aware of many sounds? Are some of them distracting? Can some of them be silenced? How can these sounds distract team members from their work?

31. **I Spy Talk**

Purpose: Communication

Group Size: 6+

Level: Basic

What do you need? No extra items are needed

How much time does it take? 10+ minutes

Description: Pick two team members and have them choose an object in the room. They cannot tell anyone what it is. They begin talking to one another about the object but never say what the object is. The team's task is to try to guess what the object is. Whoever guesses the correct object can pick a partner and choose a new item.

Was this hard to do? Did some people communicate clearer than others? Why? Was it hard to talk about something and not name what it was?

32. **I Spy Talk Alternate Version**

Description: In this version, the team leader picks an object or a subject. These do not have to be in the room. The team leader can make these as hard or easy as he or she chooses and can choose subjects that impact the team in what they do.

33. What Is My Crazy Line?

Purpose: Communication

Group Size: 4+ (in pairs)

Level: Basic

What do you need? Sentences prepared ahead of time

How much time does it take? 20+ minutes (10 minutes of prep time)

Description: The leader must develop some wacky sentences. These sentences are written on pieces of paper. One of the team pairs comes and faces one another. One of the pair is given a sentence. They must have a conversation that includes that sentence somewhere and for it to make sense. They are given a two-minute time limit. This is repeated with the other pairs. The pair that successfully does the task more times wins.

Was it difficult to control a conversation in order to use the sentence? Did you want to give up? Did you have to pick a certain subject to talk about?

34. What Is My Crazy Line Alternate Version #1

Description: In this version, the rules change a little. The pair is given the sentence and a conversation to talk about. This can be more difficult.

35. What is My Crazy Line Alternate Version #2

Description: In this version, the other member of the pair must try to identify the sentence or the theme of the conversation. There are no rules about how the pairs communicate this information.

How did the pairs let the other person know what to pay attention to? Did they change their voice, say a word, or use some other form of nonverbal communication?

36. Stickies

Purpose: Listening skills

Group Size: 6+

Level: Advanced

What do you need? Sticky notes, a card or board game of your choice

How much time does it take? 20+ minutes

Description: This is a game within a game. Team members are given three sticky notes to put on their clothes. Whenever a person talks out of turn, is not listening, or is saying something inappropriate, a sticky is taken from them by the person who noticed they were not listening. This will continue through the board game. The person with the most sticky notes in the end wins.

Discuss how it felt to give feedback to others. Did you notice you were talking out of turn?

37. Task Master

Purpose: Communication

Group Size: 6+

Level: Advanced

What do you need? No extra materials are needed

How much time does it take? 20+ minutes

Description: The first person chooses another team member and gives them a number of tasks to complete. For instance, they may say, "I want to do five tasks." The person chosen must then choose five tasks for that person to perform such as "Pick up a piece of paper, write your name on the paper, fold the paper five times, turn around three times, and unfold the paper with your eyes closed." These directions are only given once. The person must complete the tasks as given. This is a listening exercise. The winner is whoever completes the most number of tasks. The game continues until everyone has had a chance to give and perform tasks.

Did they have trouble repeating what was told to them?

38. Task Master Alternate Version

Description: In this version, the players do not only their tasks but also everyone else's tasks before them. If anyone messes up, the game begins again. This improves listening skills when other people are talking.

39. Horse Show

Purpose: Listening skills

Group Size: 8+ (enough for 4 teams)

Level: Advanced

What do you need? Small items that can be used to create four small obstacle courses. These can be cones, balls, ropes, Frisbees, or anything else. You need a large area to create 4 obstacle courses.

How much time does it take? 30+ minutes

Description: There are four groups that must create simple courses in their assigned areas. When they are complete, each team learns about the other team's course. They learn what they need to do in order to get out of the course.

Each individual will attempt to go through all four courses using the directions given. If he messes up, he must go to the back of the line to try again.

Did everyone complete it the first time through? Did people learn from other people's mistakes? Did people give clear instructions?

40. The Complete Story

Purpose: Listening skills

Group Size: 6+ (2 or more groups)

Level: Basic

What do you need? Paper and pens

How much time does it take? 20+ minutes

Description: In this exercise, the groups must come up with a story. Each person is assigned a scene in the story and should draw the scene individually. The groups come together and show their stories. If the group listened, they will understand their roles in the story.

41. The Complete Story Alternate Version #1

Description: In this version, the leader reads a story. Each person is assigned a number. The leader says the number before they read a passage from the story. The person whose number is called is assigned to draw that scene. When the story is completed, the team members must then draw their scenes. They come back together to see if they drew the scenes correctly.

42. The Complete Story Alternate Version #2

Description: In this version, the person whose scene it is must draw the scene and try to repeat his or her portion of the story. The story is then retold by the team members based upon their memory.

43. **Listen Build**

Purpose: Communication

Group Size: 6+ (2 teams)

Level: Basic

What do you need? Clay for each group

How much time does it take? 15+ minutes

Description: The members of the two teams face their backs to one another. The first team creates a sculpture out of the clay. They must then describe it to the other team so that they can recreate the same sculpture on their side.

This is repeated for the other side. Then the teams can look and see how they did.

Was it hard to describe things to others? Did people interpret what they heard differently?

44. **Listen Build Alternate Version #1**

Description: In this version, a painting is created. This task is harder because a painting is harder to correct. The teams must communicate clearly and listen before they attempt to recreate the painting.

Was it harder with paint or clay? Did everyone participate and help guide the painter? Did everyone have a different vision?

45. **Listen Build Alternate Version #2**

Description: In this version, the leader creates a sculpture out of colored clay. The leader then gives each team the same colored clay and describes the sculpture for both teams at the same time. The final sculptures are compared.

Did the groups take a different approach? Did the groups do the same sculpture or were they different?

46. **What Swims?**

Purpose: Listening skills

Group Size: 3+

Level: Basic

What do you need? No extra materials are needed

How much time does it take? 15+ minutes

Description: This game is similar to Simon Says. The leader says a list of animals that swim, like "fish swim, dolphins swim, people swim, anteaters swim." During the calling of the animals everyone is doing a swimming motion. When the leader reaches an animal that does not usually swim, such as an anteater, everyone must stop swimming. Whoever continues is out until there is one person left. The leader can choose to use other verbs such as crawl, jump, and hop instead of swim. The leader can also use other team members to call out names.

47. **Directionless Paper Planes**

Purpose: Listening skills

Group Size: 3+

Level: Basic

What do you need? Paper

How much time does it take? 10+ minutes

Description: The team leader makes a paper airplane where the team cannot see it. The leader describes what he is doing and the team members must fold the paper airplane the same way. When the leader is finished, everyone should compare his or her planes. The leader can choose someone else to make a plane and explain it to others.

Was it hard not to watch the process when making the plane? How many people were able to complete the planes?

48. **Wordless Paper Animal**

Purpose: Nonverbal skills

Group Size: 3+

Level: Advanced

What do you need? Paper, and the ability to make an origami animal or paper airplane.

How much time does it take? 10+ minutes

Description: The leader or another team member must get in front of the team and demonstrate how to fold the paper to create a plane or an origami animal. The rule is that they cannot say a word. If they see someone struggling, they can only unfold and refold to show the team member. Each team member should be given a chance to demonstrate a paper creation.

Was this hard to do without talking? Did some people do better seeing the object or hearing about how it was made? Was it hard to teach without using words?

49. **Mirror Dance**

Purpose: Nonverbal skills

Group Size: 4+

Level: Basic

What do you need? No extra materials are needed

How much time does it take? 10+ minutes

Description: The leader or other team member must demonstrate a simple dance or body movement. He cannot say anything, and can only use his body. He can repeat the movement only twice. The other team members must duplicate the dance. Every team member should be given a chance to demonstrate his or her own movement.

Was it hard to follow without words? Did you need to see the dance a couple more times to commit the movement to memory?

50. Follow the Beat

Purpose: Listening skills

Group Size: 3+

Level: Basic

What do you need? A drum, but is not necessary

How much time does it take? 5+ minutes

Description: This exercise is simple. The leader starts off by striking a simple beat. The group repeats that beat by hitting it on their table or leg. The leader then does another beat, and the team must repeat the pattern. The leader can make the beat more and more complicated. Everyone should have a turn leading the team.

Was it hard to repeat what was heard? Did you follow your neighbor's lead? Did you want the pattern repeated?

51. What's Wrong With This Picture?

Purpose: Visual skills

Group Size: 4+

Level: Basic

What do you need? No extra materials are needed

How much time does it take? 10+ minutes

Description: Have the team look at you very closely. Then leave the room and change something on your clothing. When you return, have the team decide what is changed. Have them come up with a group answer. Do this a few times; each time make it harder for them to spot.

Did it take a lot of concentration? Were some people better at the task than others?

52. What's Wrong With This Picture? Alternate Version

Description: In this version, have team look hard at the room. Have them leave and change one item around and then let the team back in to see if they can spot it. You can try to change more than one item and see how many things the team catches.

53. Can You Follow Directions?

Purpose: Listening skills

Group Size: 4+ (two groups)

Level: Basic

What do you need? Paper and pen

How much time does it take? 10+ minutes

Description: Write down ten different sets of instructions on separate pieces of paper. Make the directions no more than three steps long. Give each team five sets of directions. Have the team read the directions one at a time to the other team. They must only say the directions once. Once they read the directions, the other team has to do what the directions said. Then it is their turn to read directions to the other team. Do this until all 10 directions have been read. The group with the most successful demonstration of the directions wins.

Here are some sample sets of instructions:

- Get up. Turn around. Shake the person's hand to your left.

- Hop on one foot. Lock elbows with your teammates. Do a chorus line.

- Nod your head twice. Laugh once. Nod your head eight times.

Was it hard to hear the directions only once? Did you get the directions right but out of order? Did the entire team agree on what they heard before the team executed the directions?

54. Can You Follow Directions? Advanced Version

Description: In this version, the groups come up with the directions. They should be only three steps to start with. Then begin adding steps. The team that can do the most steps without a mistake wins.

Was it harder with more steps? How did they remember all of the steps? Was there a method of remembering them?

55. Today's Word Is

Purpose: Communication

Group Size: 6+

Level: Advanced

What do you need? No extra materials are needed

How much time does it take? 20+ minutes

Description: One of the team members is asked to leave the room. The team leader tells the rest of the team a word that they cannot say but will try to get the team member that is outside the room to say.

The team member comes back into the room and the team begins talking to him. They are trying to get the team member to say the word; meanwhile the team member needs to talk while trying to avoid using the word. Once the member says the word, another team member leaves the room and a new word is chosen.

How did it feel for the team members to know something you did not? How did it feel to try to avoid saying something when you did not know what it was? How did it feel to be a team member trying to get the team member to do something but not tell them directly?

56. **Money, Money, Who's Got Three Bucks?**

Purpose: Communication, problem solving

Group Size: 6+ (at least 2 groups)

Level: Basic

What do you need? 3 gold dollar coins for each group

How much time does it take? 20+ minutes

Description: In this activity, the team is given the three coins. They must decide who will get the coins and why. Give them five minutes. If they cannot negotiate who gets the coins and provide an explanation, they lose the coins.

The aim of this exercise is negotiation and problem solving. This forces the teams to come up with a solution quickly.

How did they work it out? Were team members baffled by the simplicity of the task? Did everyone negotiate?

57. **Money, Money, Who's Got Three Bucks? Alternate Version**

Description: In this version, the team must decide what team member in the other group they will split the money with and why.

How did the negotiation go with one of the team members not being part of the process? Were people afraid of hurting someone's feelings or playing favorites?

58. **Cut Me a Deal**

Purpose: Communication

Group Size: 6+ (2 groups)

Level: Basic

What do you need? A magazine with full page pictures, 2 large envelopes, scissors

How much time does it take? 30+ minutes (10 + minutes of prep time)

Description: Take about 40 picture pages and cut them diagonally so that you have four triangles for each page. Now mix up the pieces. Put half of the pictures into each envelope. Give the envelopes to each team. Give them a few minutes to figure out what they have and what they need.

Next ask the teams to work with one another to get the pieces they need. The team that ends up with the most full pictures wins. Set a time limit.

How did negotiation go? Was everyone a part of the process? What was the strategy and who came up with it? Was a good strategy?

59. **Tell Me All About It**

Purpose: Listening skills

Group Size: 4+ (in pairs)

Level: Basic

What do you need? Paper and pen

How much time does it take? 20+ minutes (15+ minutes of prep time)

Description: The leader will create simple lists of topics to talk about. Here is a sample list:

- What I ate last night
- What is my favorite movie and why
- Where I went to school
- What is my favorite book and why

Give the list to the pairs. One of the members in the pair will talk first. He will talk for five minutes while the other person listens. When he is finished the person listening must summarize what she heard in a minute. The roles are then changed. The only rule is that when you are listening you cannot talk.

Was it hard to remember what the person said? Was it difficult not to say anything?

60. **Tell Me All About It Alternate Version**

Description: In this version, the person listening is blindfolded. They must listen carefully.

Was it easier to listen when you could not see anything? Was it harder? Did you notice that the less things that distracted you, the more you were able to truly listen?

61. **There Is No "I" in Team**

Purpose: Communication

Group Size: 4+ (in pairs)

Level: Basic

What do you need? No extra materials are needed

How much time does it take? 20+ minutes

Description: In this activity, the partners sit across from one another. One is chosen to be the listener and other is chosen to be the talker. The talker must speak about a topic of their choice for two minutes without stopping. The listener must sit and listen and not say anything. The talker cannot use the word "I" at anytime. If they do, the listener must raise his or her hand and the session ends. Then they reverse roles. The pair that can get to two minutes the most times wins.

How did it feel not to use the word "I"? Was it difficult? Was it easy?

62. **What Do You Value?**

Purpose: Communication

Group Size: 6+ (2 or more groups)

Level: Advanced

What do you need? Paper, pen, poster board for each group, and markers

How much time does it take? 30+ minutes

Description: Have each team member write a list of the most important values of the team or organization to which they belong. Have the group narrow this down to the top five values. Have them list these on the poster board and decorate or color the poster to emphasize these values. When they are complete, have the team share their creation with the rest of the groups.

How did it feel to talk about group values? Were your values chosen as one of the top five? If not, how does that feel? Did you tell the group how you felt? Was it hard to pick only five values? Were there common values between the groups?

63. **Old Barrels to Sell**

Purpose: Communication

Group Size: 6+ (at least 2 groups)

Level: Advanced

What do you need? Paper and pen

How much time does it take? 30+ minutes

Description: The leader states that the group has just come across 20,000 old wooden barrels and must figure out a way to market them.

The teams are given a set amount of time to come up with a plan and a pitch for the barrels. The groups come together and share their pitches. The leader chooses the most clear and concise pitch as the winner.

How hard was it to sell that many barrels? Were there creative ideas of what they could be used for or how to sell them quickly? Was it hard to come up with a sales pitch?

64. **Dart Board**

Purpose: Deal with emotion

Group Size: 3+

Level: Advanced

What do you need? Dart board, darts (one for everyone), pens or markers, and paper

How much time does it take? 10+ minutes

Description: Set up the dart board in a safe place. Have the team members draw something that is making them angry. They can write the words or draw a picture. When everyone is finished, attach each person's picture on the board. Everyone must throw his or her dart at the picture. Once everyone has done this, the picture is torn and destroyed. The next person's picture is put up next.

How did it feel to destroy your picture? How did it fell to have others help you destroy it? How did it feel to share your feelings with the group?

65. **Burn It Away**

Purpose: Deal with emotion

Group Size: 3+

Level: Advanced

What do you need? A large ash tray, matches, paper, and pen

How much time does it take? 10+ minutes

Description: This exercise should be done outdoors and a fire extinguisher should be handy. Have team members write down what is making them feel angry or irritated that week. They should be team related but do not have to be. When everyone is finished, the team members come to the ashtray one at a time. They read what it is on the paper and say: "Burn my anger away." They light the paper and put it into the ashtray. You must wait until each paper is completely burned to ash before the next person steps up.

How did it feel to burn the paper? How did it feel to share your anger with others? How did it feel to support teammates as they burned their papers?

66. **Break It Away**

Purpose: Deal with emotion

Group Size: 3+

Level: Advanced

What do you need? Old bottles, a safe place to break bottles (see below), something to stop up the bottle like a cork, a wad of paper, or cotton, and safety goggles

How much time does it take? 10+ minutes

Description: This exercise can work well if you have access to a recycling center. You should be extremely careful doing this activity and wear safety goggles. Have each team member think about something that is making them mad or irritated. Have them yell what ever it is into the empty bottle. When they have finished their rant, have them stop up the bottle. Each team member does this until everyone has a bottle. Find a safe place to throw and break the bottles. The glass should be used for recycling, so large open recycling bins at recycling or trash centers work well. Allow each team member to hurl his or her bottle and allow the anger to break away.

67. **You Did What?**

Purpose: Communication

Group Size: 6+

Level: Advanced

What do you need? Paper, pens, and envelopes

How much time does it take? 30+ minutes

Description: Each team member will write one thing about each other team member. It can be scandalous, true, or gossip. Each item is written on a different piece of paper. Envelopes with team member's names are sent around and the team members must put the slips of paper in the appropriate envelope.

The team leader will pick someone to be first. The person chosen must sit in the center of the room. The team leader will pull a slip from the envelope. The person in the middle must guess who said it. If they get it wrong, another slip is pulled. This is continued until the person identifies the author of one of the slips. If they guess right, they sit down and the person they guessed correctly must sit in the seat. This is continued until everyone has had a chance to guess.

What did team members learn about one another? Was anyone embarrassed? Can the team see why gossip can be embarrassing?

68. **You Did What? Alternate Version**

Description: In this version, the people write the slips about themselves. The team must guess whether the statements are true or not. The team member goes through all of the slips and the one that guesses the most right gets to be the next person to sit in the seat.

Was it hard to tell truth from fiction? Did the team learn anything about one another? Did some of the lies seem like truth? Can team members see how they could believe a lie?

69. **Mini-Marshmallow Pass**

Purpose: Communication

Group Size: 6+ (in pairs)

Level: Basic

What do you need? Mini-marshmallows, spoons, and blindfolds

How much time does it take? 10+ minutes

Description: The task is for the partners to pass ten mini-marshmallows to the other person to eat. The problem is that both partners are blindfolded. They must scoop up the marshmallow on the spoon and feed it to their partner. When one partner has completed eating ten marshmallows, the partners change roles.

Was it difficult to do without the use of sight? What techniques did the partners figure out to accomplish the task? How did it feel to rely on the other person? Was it scary to be fed while blindfolded?

70. **It Is Puzzling**

    Purpose: Communication

    Group Size: 6+ (at least 2 groups)

    Level: Advanced

    What do you need? A bag and 2 to 3 children's puzzles. They should not contain more than 25 pieces each.

    How much time does it take? 30+ minutes

    Description: The team leader mixes the pieces of the different puzzles. The team does not know this. He then gives each group a bag of pieces. The task is simple; they must complete their puzzle (you may decide to give them a time limit).

    The groups will figure out that they have the wrong pieces. If they ask the leader, the leader should just repeat that they need to complete the task. They should say no more.

    Did the groups figure out what to do? Did they do it on their own? Did any puzzle get completed? Were team members afraid of taking initiative?

71. The New Break Room

Purpose: Communication

Group Size: 6+ (at least 2 teams)

Level: Advanced

What do you need? Paper and markers

How much time does it take? 20+ minutes

Description: In this activity, the groups are told that they can design a new breakroom. There is no budget, so the sky is the limit. They are to draw it and be ready to share it with the team. The rule is that no one can talk during the activity. There should be a time limit. The team with the most complete design wins.

How did team members communicate? Was it difficult? Did they run out of time? Was it difficult not being able to talk? Did everyone agree on the design? How do you know?

72. Fix It

Purpose: Communication

Group Size: 4+

Level: Advanced

What do you need? Blocks and a stopwatch

How much time does it take? 15+ minutes

Description: The leader will stack the blocks in a random way on the table and announce that the team will have to "fix" the stack in 60 seconds. The leader will say "go." The team will have to interpret what "fix" means. If they ask the leader for clarification, the leader will only repeat the instructions.

Would this be easier if you had better instructions? Did the team give up? Did the team develop a quick strategy?

73. Fix It Alternate Version

Description: Instead of blocks, the leader will hand the group a page-long excerpt from a magazine, paper, or newsletter. The instruction will be the same: "fix it." The leader can add spelling or grammatical errors to the passage to help the process.

Was it hard to find what was wrong with the passage? Did the team choose what to do? Did one person make corrections or was it a group effort?

74. Group Story

Purpose: Teamwork

Group Size: 4+

Level: Basic

What do you need? Paper and pen

How much time does it take? 10+ minutes

Description: The task is for the team to create a story. Each person will say a word to keep the story going. The story will begin with "Once" and the story will end with "end." The story continues through each team member until the story is ended.

It is optional for the leader to write the story as it is being told. It can be fun to hear the story in its entirety.

Was it hard to say just one word? Did you want to steer the story in a particular direction? Was it frustrating to be given a word that was hard to follow up with or was not the word you wanted the previous person to say?

75. Group Story Alternate Version #1

Description: In this version, the group must create a story about the team. They must tell about how the team was created and what great things the team has accomplished.

Was telling a story with a purpose more difficult? Did it make the story longer? Did the leader finally have to end it? Was it hard not to have decided what would be included before the story began?

76. Group Story Alternate Version #2

Description: In this version, the story must include each team member. The team member must have a name that describes them. Here are examples:

John the muffin eater

Jane the do righter

Sam the silly driver

Did any of the names make people mad? Was this harder to do? Did it stop the story when people had to come up with a descriptive name?

77. Card Shuffle

Purpose: Communication

Group Size: 5+

Level: Basic

What do you need? A deck of cards and a stopwatch

How much time does it take? 10+ minutes

Description: In this activity, the team leader mixes a deck of cards up. The group must get the cards in order by ace to king; the order of the suits is spades, clubs, hearts, and diamonds. They have 90 seconds to do this.

Was it hard to complete? Did it take the whole team to complete? Could one person do it? Did it take a few tries to complete?

78. **Card Shuffle Alternate Version**

Description: In this version, the team is broken up into groups. Each group is given 13 cards. They can be any 13 cards. Each team is assigned a suit that they must complete. They must negotiate with the other groups to complete their task. The time limit is two minutes.

Was this hard to complete? What was the strategy? How were cards negotiated? Were people assigned to find certain cards? Was it a team effort to complete? Did it take more than one try to complete?

79. **No Buts About It, Only Ifs or Ands**

Purpose: Communication

Group Size: 4+ (in pairs)

Level: Advanced

What do you need? No extra materials are needed

How much time does it take? 10+ minutes

Description: Team members must think of one thing they like and one think they dislike about the team. The partners must state their two statements to one another. The second statement must start with the word "but". Here is an example:

"I like the humor of the team. But we need longer lunch breaks."

Once each person says the two sentences, have him repeat them using the word "and."

Here is an example: "I like the humor of the group and we need longer lunch breaks."

How did the feeling of the statement change? Did the word "but" feel different than the word "and?" How can this be used in the team's communications?

80. No Buts About It, Only Ifs or Ands Alternate Version #1

Description: In this version, the words "yes but" are used. The theme of the conversation is a team retreat. In this exercise each team member makes a suggestion about the retreat. The other team member replies with "yes but" to begin his sentence. Here is an example:

"I hope we get to eat Italian."

"Yes but I hope we get a day off."

"Yes but I want to go swimming."

Now the partners exchange the words "yes but" with the word "and"

"I hope we get to eat Italian."

"And I hope we get a day off."

"And I want to go swimming."

Did the change in two words change the meaning and feeling of the statements?

81. No Buts About It, Only Ifs or Ands Alternative Version #2

Description: In this version, the partners discuss problems in the team. The partner responds with "but you," Here is an example:

"The team does not have enough time to get anything done."

"But you work overtime on weekends a lot."

"But you would like to take longer lunch breaks."

Now the partners must change the words to "I."

"The team does not have enough time to get anything done."

"I work overtime on weekends a lot."

"I would like to take longer lunch breaks."

How did the feeling of the statements make the partners feel? Did "but you" make them defensive? Did using the word "I" give the person more ownership over the issue?

82. **What Do You Think of Her?**

Purpose: First Impressions

Group Size: 6+

Level: Advanced

What do you need? Pictures, pens, paper

How much time does it take? 20+ minutes (20+ minutes of prep time)

Description: The leader should do some research and find ten different pictures of unknown people. The leader must find professionals and people from different occupations and know what they do for a living, or something that they accomplished that was important.

The leader will give the pictures to the group and the team must write down their impressions of the person and what they think they do for a living. When the team has seen all of the pictures, the team should share their impressions. The leader will then tell the team who the person really is. The person with the most correct guesses wins.

What did people get from first impressions? Is it fair to judge someone on how they look? Did it change the team's opinions when they heard who the people were?

83. What Do You Think of Her? Alternate Version #1

Description: In this version, the team is given a list of descriptions about the people. They must match the person to the brief description.

Was this easier to do? Were there surprises? Did anyone get all of them correct?

84. What Do You Think of Her? Alternate Version #2

Description: In this version, the leader collects pictures of members of the organization, not on the team, when they were babies. The pictures are shown to the group and they must write down their impressions of the children and guess who they grew up to be.

Were certain people easy to guess? What signs were there of who they were? Have people changed a lot since they were children?

85. True Colors

Purpose: Getting to know your team

Group Size: 4+

Level: Advanced

What do you need? Many different colored markers or crayons

How much time does it take? 15+ minutes

Description: The leader picks a different colored marker for each team member. The team members must find someone else that has a similar colored marker. They have 60 seconds to find something they have in common with that person.

The team members should then find someone with a totally different color than their own. In 60 seconds they should find a subject they have totally different views on. The team should come back together and share their results.

Even though there are differences, is there a healthy diversity in the group? Is diversity good?

86. **True Colors Alternate Version**

Description: In this version, the team members pick their own colors. The exercise is the same except they must explain why the color represents them.

Were people's explanation of the colors similar or were people's explanations vastly different if the colors were different?

87. **Definitions**

Purpose: Getting to know your team

Group Size: 4+

Level: Advanced

What do you need? Index cards and pens

How much time does it take? 20+ minutes

Description: Each team member is given five cards. They must write what an effective leader is. Each card will contain a different aspect of what makes a good leader.

The team leader will collect and shuffle all of the cards. She will add her own set of cards to the stack. The leader will then deal out three cards to each team member. They must rank the cards according what they believe are important aspects of a good leader.

The leader will then place the remaining cards on a table and the team members may select cards to trade. They must have three cards when they are finished trading. No one can talk during this stage of the exercise. The object is to have three cards that are the closest to what they believe makes a good leader.

The team members are then allowed to trade cards. Again the idea is to have the best three cards possible. The leader should give them a time limit.

Have the team members share their cards and state why they feel that these three represent what they believe a good leader is.

How did they feel about the card they were left with? Did teammates agree with each other about what aspects make a good leader?

88. Definitions Alternate Version

Description: In this version, the team will define what makes an effective team. The team will choose as they did before. When they have all of their cards, the leader will take them away and allow the team members to pick two cards from what is left. Each team member must state why these cards are important. The people who wrote the card must identify themselves and explain what they wrote.

How did it feel to have your choices taken away? Were the choices that were left good ideas? Why or why not? Why would others list these cards along with the ones they created?

89. Draw a Bunny or Else

Purpose: Communication

Group Size: 6+ (the team may need to be split into smaller groups)

Level: Advanced

What do you need? Paper, pen, and stopwatch

How much time does it take? 20+ minutes

Description: In this exercise, the leader picks a coach for the team. The team sits in front of the piece of paper and pen. The leader now gives the following instructions:

"The coach is responsible for the team to follow my instructions and complete the task. Everyone but the coach should now close his or her eyes. With your pen, you are to draw a bunny. This bunny will have a head and a body. Nothing else is to be drawn. You have two minutes. Remember, coach, it is your job to make sure the task is completed."

Give the team about two minutes to complete the task.

"The coach once again will make sure you complete this task. Keep your eyes closed. The task is to draw a cotton tail and ears on the bunny. Remember, coach, you must make sure your team completes this task. You have three minutes. Go."

Have everyone open their eyes and see their creations. How did the coach feel to be responsible for the task? How did she work it out? Did the team members listen and wait or try to do it themselves?

90. **Draw a Bunny or Else Alternate Version**

Description: In this version the team is creating cookies while their eyes are closed.

Here are the steps:

1. Cut the shape from the dough

2. Ice the cookies

3. Decorate the cookies with sprinkles

4. Put cookies on cookie sheet

When you are finished, you can eat the cookies.

Was this hard to complete? Did the task require more than one coach? Did everyone listen? Was there a plan to get the steps done?

91. Move Me

Purpose: Communication

Group Size: 4+

Level: Advanced

What do you need? Paper, pen

How much time does it take? 20+ minutes

Description: On paper, have the team write what kind of motivation they prefer. They should list at least ten different kinds.

The leader should then discuss the two main types of motivation, the kind we get from other people and the kind we find within ourselves. Have the team go over their lists and decide what kinds of motivation they have listed. Have the team members add the two types together and report to the group which kind they prefer.

Did people learn from one another? Were people surprised by their own answers? Were people surprised by other people's answers?

92. The Three Monkeys

Purpose: Communication

Group Size: 6+

Level: Advanced

What do you need? Blindfold, simple office objects such as a pen, stapler, markers, or paper clip

How much time does it take? 20+ minutes

Description: The objects are set on one side of the room. Two team members are chosen to help. Team member 1 is blindfolded and placed near the objects. Team member 2 is placed in the center of the room. And the rest of the team is at the far end of the room. Here are the rules:

Team member 1 can talk but cannot see.

Team member 2 can see and talk but can only look at the team members on the far side of the room.

The remaining team members can see but not speak. Team member 2 must direct team member 1, according to what the other team members convey.

The team leader gives a task that team member 1 must accomplish, but only shows it to the mute team members. The game is completed when team member 1 finishes the task. Different team members may try other roles with new tasks.

How did it feel to be team member 1? How about team member 2? How did it feel to be in the mute crowd? Was it a team effort to accomplish the task? What strategies were used?

93. **The Right Question**

   Purpose: Communication

   Group Size: 4+ (in pairs)

   Level: Basic

   What do you need? No additional materials are needed

   How much time does it take? 20+ minutes

Description: The leader will explain the difference between open and closed questions. Open questions allow the person to explain their answer. Here is an example: What types of food do you like? A closed question usually requires a one-word answer like "yes" or "no". Here is an example: Do you like Italian food?

One person in the pair is given a scenario. Here is an example:

The person is going on a vacation to Disneyworld. He is bringing his family and they are staying for three days. They are going to visit the Magic Kingdom, Epcot, and MGM Studios.

The other partner will be given two minutes to figure out what the scenario is. They can only use closed-ended questions. Both of the partners try to figure out scenarios using only closed-ended questions.

After both partners have a chance to ask a question, the leader will give them new scenarios. This time they can only use open-ended questions. Again, they will be given two minutes to figure out the scenario.

What type of questions were easier to use? Were you able to discover the scenario quicker by using open-ended questions? Would a mix of the two have made it easier?

94. Mediator

Purpose: Mediation skills

Group Size: 6+ (2 or more groups)

Level: Advanced

What do you need? Newspaper

How much time does it take? 20+ minutes

Description: The group finds a controversial subject in the newspaper. They work as a team to come up with a solution to the problem. Here are questions that the group has to answer:

- What questions could be asked of the parties involved to work toward an agreeable solution?

- What can be changed about the situation that could prevent it from happening in the future?

- What is each side's main complaints, feelings, needs, and motivators?

- How could the problem have been averted or predicted?

- How can others in similar situations learn from this?

Give the groups a deadline. Have the groups reconvene and share their issue and how they resolved the problem by answering the five questions.

Did everyone participate in coming up with solutions? Did everyone agree on the solution? Did the group take a vote?

95. Mediator Alternate Version #1

Description: In this version, one person from the team is chosen to be the mediator. The rest of the team is divided, each group supporting one side of the problem. They should role play and the mediator must try to resolve the dispute. Different scenarios can be used with each mediator.

How did it feel to mediate? Did you do it successfully?

96. Mediator Alternate Version #2

Description: In this version, the scenario is the same as in alternate version #1 except that when the team leader taps the mediator on the shoulder, the mediator must switch places with another team member. The mediation continues where it left off.

How did it feel to be on one side of an issue and then have to look at both sides equally? Did it give you a new perspective?

97. Were You Paying Attention?

Purpose: Observation skills

Group Size: 6+ (2 or more groups)

Level: Advanced

What do you need? Flip chart, simple objects around the room such as balls, pens, paper, etc.

How much time does it take? 20+ minutes

Description: During another exercise or when the team enters the room, have a set of instructions on a flip chart. It should be no more than five steps. Do not say anything about the instructions, just have them in a visible location.

Begin the exercise by taking away the instructions. Break the team up into groups. Tell the groups that they have one task and that is to complete the instructions that you just removed. Team members will have to rely on memory and communication to complete the task. Give the team five minutes to complete it. The team that most closely completes the task wins.

Were you paying attention? Did people have different recollections of the instructions? Was there a consensus?

98. Were You Paying Attention? Alternate Version

Description: In this version, have the instructions where the group can see them. Be sure to include instructions that say they must start the exercise when you leave the room. One of the first steps is for the team to leave the room to retrieve an item. While they are gone, remove the instructions. When they return they must continue exercise by memory.

Did anyone think to write down the instructions? Were the teams so competitive that they did not take time to plan? Did it mean losing in the end?

99. **Does This Make Sense?**

Purpose: Communication

Group Size: 4+ (in pairs)

Level: Basic

What do you need? Paper with the message below

How much time does it take? 10 minutes

Description: The team leader reads the following passage.

"Seeb klat without gniyas a drow! Did you know that when seeb move they etacinummoc to each other through dance. Their dance is one way they klat or etacinummoc about flowers."

The leader asks what the passage means. No one will probably be able to give an answer. Give the pairs a copy of the passage. The pair that deciphers it first wins.

Is clear communication valuable? Is there more than one way to communicate? Are some ways better in certain situations?

100. **What Is Inside**

Purpose: Decision making

Group Size: 5+

Level: Basic

What do you need? 2 boxes and wrapping paper

How much time does it take? 10+ minutes

Description: The leader should nicely wrap one box with a bow.

The second box should be wrapped sloppily and torn.

The leader holds up the first box and asks who would choose that gift. And then ask the same about the second gift. The leader should ask the team members why they chose a particular box. Do people choose things based upon how they look rather than what is inside? What about food choices? What about packaging of toys and cereal? Do people make judgments about others based upon how they look and what they wear?

5

Self-Esteem & Self-Discovery Activities

Teambuilding activities that challenge participants to get outside their comfort zone are great at building self-esteem. These challenges tend to be physically demanding, like walking on a log 30 feet in the air while attached to a belay or moving each member of the group through a "spider's web." The transformation of the individual from being timid about the activity to the huge smile and excitement of accomplishing the task is awesome.

Deb Dowling

Rather than starting with the thought, "Let's have a teambuilding event," organizations should work backward from what areas of the business need improvement toward, "Should an event be held and if so what does it look like?"

Breon Klopp

Creating new challenges helps team members work together to meet the challenges, and tighter bonds of trust are formed. Teams learn what they are made of. A sense of ownership and pride develops. They feel like they can accomplish things together and each success builds upon previous successes.

Pramod Goel believes that self-esteem and self-discovery are exposed more during a team activity in a controlled and simulated environment. He has made the following observations:

- One person always thought he was a fast worker and did a quality job, but when he worked in the controlled team environment he realized that he had an impact on the whole process flow. He was able to compare his speed and the quality of his work with others on the team, and determine whether he was holding the line or making it easy for everyone to succeed.

- People realized that, if they remained calm when things were not going right, it had an impact on others.

Self-esteem and self-discovery are important in a team that functions well. If the individual feels good about what they are doing and accomplishing, both individually and as part of a larger team, they will be more motivated to not only continue their hard work and dedication, but will strive to accomplish even more.

It is up to the leader to monitor how members of the team are doing. This can be done in a variety of ways.

Depending on the work circumstance and the type of team, checking in can be a very powerful technique. A check-in by the leader of the group can be daily, weekly, or monthly. The more frequent the check, the more effective it can be. During the check-in, the leader should start off with a positive remark like: "You really went above and beyond the call of duty yesterday" or "I was really impressed with how you dealt with your team member during the crisis today."

This sets the stage as a positive one, rather than a negative one. This can be followed by something that needs to be worked on. Your statement should still start off with a positive. For example:

"I have noticed you are not pulling your load. You are really adding to your team members' workload."

This is the better statement: "I noticed you have been working hard at your job. Have you considered trying to speed up your production? It will help your coworkers and maybe they can help you with some of your other duties."

As you can see, you are including them in a team, rather than singling them out as an individual. They can identify as a team member. It is helpful if team members understand that they are responsible and an important member of a team rather than just having personal responsibility. It is easier to make excuses for our own individual mistakes than to let down others on a team.

Being part of a successful team can be a powerful feeling. In 1943, a well-known psychologist Abraham Maslow published a groundbreaking study called *A Theory of Human Motivation*. In the paper, Maslow suggested what has become known as the hierarchy of needs. This pyramid contains a set of human needs that motivates human beings and accounts for many human behaviors.

Here is a list of needs, from basic to higher psychological needs. Maslow suggests that every human has this same pyramid of needs and that we can jump from one level to another at different times.

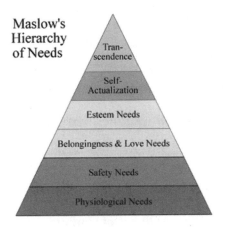

Maslow suggests that, if the first four needs are not met, we feel anxious. The reason this is included in this book is that members of your team are affected daily by every one of these needs. If you can recognize symptoms of deficiency, you can help your team members get back on track. If these needs are not met, humans become distracted and focus on their needs until they are met. The following pages give a description of the levels.

Physiological

These needs are basic, physical needs. They include food, drink, sleep, and sex. These change throughout the day and have to be met before we can do or think about anything else. If you have a team member who is hungry, he will focus on eating and where he is going to lunch rather than his job assignment. Make sure that your team has snacks available and breaks. If you see team members who are tired or not taking breaks, insist that they do. If they are tired, their production will drop. It is much better that they go home for the day or take a break than to continue to work while tired. This is also a risk for their safety and those around them if they are sleep deprived. If you are a manager, consider this factor before scheduling too many double shifts for team members.

Beyond these physical needs, it is recommended that you include a health program for your team. This would include diet suggestions and exercise. Consider what your team members are buying from vending machines. You can develop a plan to offer healthy snacks to employees.

Many companies are finding huge benefits in offering exercise programs to their employees. Giving team members time to exercise or even offering an exercise program has the following benefits:

- Team members are healthier. They are more productive and miss less work. This saves money. They also use their insurance less because they are not visiting the doctor as often. This translates into huge savings for a company.

- Team members are in better condition. They have fewer accidents and are able to perform physical tasks quicker and easier.

- Team members are more alert and less tired. They have clearer discussions and a more positive mood and attitude. There are less conflicts between team members.

Safety

Once a person's physiological needs are met, his focus will turn toward safety issues. Being safe from crime and harm is the central theme of this need. Your team members must feel safe and that you are taking their safety concerns into account. If they do not feel safe, they will become anxious and scared. They will not feel like the team is protecting them. I once worked at an agency where my team members often worked after hours. There was no safety light in the parking lot, and this became a major issue because the team did not feel safe. Fortunately, the team leader heard their concerns and not only added motion detecting lights, but also a security system that locked the door behind you after you entered the building.

Safety also includes security. If there are a lot of layoffs and turnover in a company, the team members may not feel as though they are secure in their jobs. This goes back to hiring the right people to begin with. If the right people are part of the team, there is less likelihood of staff turnover. Keep an open door policy to allow your team members to express their concerns and help them process their fears. Team members will feel safer and more secure if they feel they are being heard.

Having a safe work environment is important. If team members feel that they can potentially get hurt while working or if there is a high incidence of accidents, team members will feel anxious and fearful.

Love/Belonging

Once a person's safety concerns are relieved they will begin to focus on social issues. This is one of the most important aspects of the team. The team fulfills this need everyday. If a person works alone, they cannot have this need fulfilled in the workplace. They can become bitter, distrustful, and unfriendly. However, if this need is met, they will feel fulfilled and part of a greater whole.

Under this need, friendship, sexual intimacy, and having a supportive and communicative network are important. Humans need a sense of belonging to a group. We are social creatures. Humans need to love and be loved. Without this we cannot function. It is as important as eating and sleeping. This is very evident in babies. Some babies suffer from a disorder called failure to thrive. In this disorder, babies are small and underweight. One of the reasons is lack of proper stimulation. Babies need touch from other humans to grow properly. This stimulation helps neuropathways form in the brain.

As a member of a team, physical touch may not be appropriate, but letting someone know you care about them as a human and as a member of a team can be a very powerful thing. People will feel that they are being heard and that they can rely on others in times of need and crisis. Without this sense of belonging, anxiety, depression, and withdrawal can occur. As a team leader, you can give people the positive regard they need daily. This boosts a person's sense of self-worth and belonging.

Self-Esteem

Humans have a need to be respected, to have self-esteem, and to have self-respect. These needs are usually met by external forces. Being part of a team can help meet this need, and you can praise and give a person all the respect in the world but, if they suffer from low self-esteem, it will have little effect. Unless you are trained as a counselor, it is not recommended that you go into depth with a team member about their self-esteem issues. You can gently push them in the direction of getting professional help. If a person is depressed and has low self-esteem, they can drag down the morale of the entire team.

Recognizing team members' accomplishments both in private and publicly can help boost a person's self-esteem. A person's self-esteem can improve her relationship with other members of the team, thus increasing the team's self-esteem.

Self-Actualization

If your team can reach this stage of need, you will have a highly functioning, motivated, and healthy team. This is not a basic need, but it is a psychological state of being. People that have reached this level have embraced the facts and realities of the world. They do not blame others and accept the way things are. They are often creative and spontaneous in their ideas and actions.

People that have reached self-actualization are interested in solving team problems. They focus on making the team the best it can be. They are solution-based and are self-motivated for the good of the team.

Teams that are self-actualized are often have a pleasant and positive outlook on work and life in general. They embrace the values and ethics of the team. They act according to what is right, regardless of what authorities may demand. They have a highly developed sense of what is right.

A team that is self-actualized is able to observe situations objectively, find solutions quickly, and act on them. They have achieved their fullest potential. That does not mean there is not room for improvement; they meet challenges easily and objectively and can shift to meet the needs of the team without being formally directed to do so.

In short, self-actualization is reaching one's fullest potential.

Transcendence

This is sometimes called spiritual needs. These are only mentioned here as reference to Maslow's complete pyramid of needs.

On the following pages you'll find activities that focus on your team's self-esteem and self-discovery.

1. Tip Me Over

Purpose: Trust and support

Group Size: 6+ (at least two groups)

Level: Advanced

What do you need? No extra materials are required

How much time does it take? 10+ minutes

Description: Break the team into two groups. The groups should form two parallel lines that are facing one another. They need to be close enough to touch their hands with the group in front of them. Have everyone hold up his or her right hand. Have each member touch hands, palm against palm, with the person standing in front of him. Do not lock fingers. Now have the team members hold up their left hands. Have them touch palms with the person on the left of the person in front of them. There will be people on the end of the rows that will only be using one hand. Now have everyone take a step back. They should be leaning forward to be supported by the people in front of them. If you want to challenge them further, have them step back again. Their legs should be straight, no bent knees are allowed. Have them step forward again before releasing hands or people might fall forward.

Discuss with the group how it felt to rely on others. Did they trust others to hold them up and support them? How did the people on the ends feel about only using one hand? If you would like, you could switch people around so different people are on the ends.

2. Shop or Else

Purpose: Communication and teamwork

Group Size: 4+

Level: Advanced

What do you need? A catalog of a variety of items or a computer with Internet access.

How much time does it take? 30+ minutes

Description: Tell the team the following story:

"You have been chosen to go to an underground bunker. It is hundreds of feet below the earth's surface. You will have enough food and water for a year. At the end of the year, you will be able to go back to the surface of the earth. During the year, you will only have two sets of clothes a piece. You have $250 to spend on anything else you will need for the year. You will only be able to bring what you buy. You have to use the money to buy supplies for everyone on the team. You cannot go over budget."

Give the team the catalog or allow them to access a store's Internet site such as Wal-Mart, Sears, or Target.

Discuss how it felt to shop for the group rather than meeting their own needs. How was the decision made to buy the items? Was everyone given an allotment to spend for himself or herself? Did they have to vote on what was bought?

3. **Fearless Factor**

   Purpose: Teamwork

   Group Size: 6+ (at least 2 teams)

   Level: Advanced

   What do you need? This depends on the challenges that are set by the teams. Try to limit the materials to items that are nearby. You do need pen and paper for each team.

   How much time does it take? 30+ minutes

   Description: Each team must come up with six challenges that they can accomplish and win. The team coming up with the challenge must be able to do the challenge before they can add it to the list for another group to accomplish. Here are some categories of possible challenges:

- Physical challenges. These are challenges that the group can do as a group, such as each member jumping rope ten times without tripping or stopping.

- Nonphysical challenges according to who is in your group. An example is that everyone can sing the happy birthday song in Spanish.

- Gross challenges (like the game show *Fear Factor*). Do not make the activities too gross or people will get sick. This one will take some pre planning. You can do things such as eating ice cream with mustard and ketchup.

The groups hand in their lists. The leader calls out a challenge and the team that created it must be able to demonstrate it. The challenges cannot be something that no other team can do. The other teams have the chance to do the challenge. If they can successfully do it, they get a point. The leader goes through all of the challenges. The team with the most points wins.

Discuss with the team how they came up with the challenges. How did the group cooperate to accomplish the challenge? Did the group members rely on the other people in their group to meet the challenge? Did they feel confident in their other team members for various challenges? Did some people have special talents that others did not?

4. **Falling Off**

Purpose: Self-discovery and trust building

Group Size: 5+

Level: Advanced

What do you need? A step stool or something to stand on

How much time does it take? 10 to 15 minutes (10 minutes of conversation)

Description: Have one person stand on a step stool; his hips should be about shoulder height of the average height of the group. Have everyone else stand behind the stool in two lines with their hands extended opposite side, forming a "basket." Have the person on the stool fall backward into the arms of the group. Remember, the taller the stool, the heavier the person will feel. Lead a conversation about trusting oneself and one's group.

5. What Animal Are You?

Purpose: Teamwork

Group Size: 4+ (for larger groups this can be broken into groups of 4)

Level: Advanced

What do you need? Large pieces of paper, art supplies (colored pencils and pens, glue, glitter, fabric material, etc.)

How much time does it take? 20+ minutes

Description: The team is broken up into smaller groups if necessary. They must pretend that they have a large farm full of animals. They have to name the farm, and each member must pick an animal or person on the farm. They must add that person or animal to the picture. Allow enough time for each group to finish. Then, have a discussion about the picture they created and allow each member to discuss why they picked a certain animal or person on the farm. You do not need to limit them to traditional farm animals; they can pick any animal they wish as long as they can draw a habitat for that animal. Discuss with the group what they learned from the activity and then ask if anyone would change who or what they picked. Finally, ask about the name of the farm and why they chose it.

It is always important to ask participants how the activity went for them. Discussion after an exercise is key. The group leader may feel as though the exercise was a success based on viewing the exercise at the time. But everyone has her or his own perspective and, while someone may have participated in the exercise, that same person may not feel that, for them, the exercise was worthwhile. It is a simple thing, but just asking participants what they got out of an exercise can lead to all sorts of great discussion and become a teambuilding exercise in and of itself.

Kim Stinson

---

6. Bus Stop

Purpose: Teamwork

Group Size: 3+

Level: Advanced

What do you need? A couple of seats to serve as a bench, and paper slips with different personality traits and conflicts written on them

How much time does it take? 20 to 30 minutes (15 minutes of prep time, 20 minutes of discussion)

Description: Have the first person pick a slip of paper. On the paper are character traits and a conflict.

Example: You are a pregnant woman and need to get to the hospital. You are having contractions. Or maybe: You are an old man that is lost and forgets where he lives. You are agitated.

The situations can also be real work situations. Each person draws a slip, reads it, and then adds it to the scene. They do not let the others know what it says, but act out their character. Each of the others must figure out a way to deal with the new situations as they arise. When everyone has had a turn, stop the scene. Make sure you discuss what you learned from the scene.

Any teambuilding exercise is a moment for building self-esteem or can lead to self-discovery. It can also do the opposite. The leader needs to be constantly aware of the dynamics in the room. If there are people who constantly hang out together in a clique, break them up into different groups. Get team members to work together who maybe don't usually hang out together around the proverbial water cooler. This way, everyone gets a chance to know everyone else better, which can lead to understanding and appreciation of differences. As a team leader, you also need to watch out for those who don't "buy in" to the concept of teambuilding exercises. Try not to force them with threats, but find ways to convince them it's a good idea to at least try. Also, try to stay away from "touchy-feely" exercises as that makes some people feel uncomfortable.

Kim Stinson

---

7. **Key People**

Purpose: Getting to know your team

Group Size: 9+

Level: Advanced

What do you need? Paper and pens

How much time does it take? 50+ minutes

Description: Break the team into three small groups. Have the groups identify key people on the team or organization. These are people who are essential and that provide necessary support and resources to the team. Give them about 5 to 10 minutes to complete this.

Have the team come back together and vote on the top three

people from the lists who are the key people on the team. This is not a popularity contest; rather, these people hold positions or do work that is essential for others to do their work.

Assign one person to each of the small groups. Read (or give a copy) of the following questions for each group to answer about the key person they have chosen. Give them about 30 minutes to complete the assignment. At the end of the allotted time, have the team reconvene and share what the groups came up with. Allow time for discussion.

1. Why is this key person so important?

2. What does the key person do for other members of the team?

3. What does the key person need from team members to perform his or her job?

4. What are the common goals that the team shares with the key person?

5. What happens when the team does not work well with the person?

6. How can a team member build a positive and successful relationship with the key person?

7. What benefit is there to having a positive relationship with the key person?

8. What happens when the key person is not available or is missing from work?

9. What kind of feedback does the key person give to team members? How can this be improved?

10. What kind of feedback are team members giving the key person? How can this be improved?

8. Fortune Teller

Purpose: Getting to know your team

Group Size: 4+

Level: Advanced

What do you need? A deck of tarot cards. You can by these at any large bookstore for about $20. Find a deck that has simple pictures.

How much time does it take? 20+ minutes

Description: Shuffle the deck well. Hand out 5 cards to each team member and put the deck in the middle of the team. Have members pick a card that most closely represents how they feel about the team. Have them select a second card. This one represents the way they want the team to be in the future. Each member has the chance to return one of his cards to the bottom of the deck and select a replacement from the top of the deck. When everyone has chosen their 2 cards, convene as a large group again. Have the members share their card selections and explain why they chose the cards they did.

9. Fortune Teller Alternate Version #1

Description: In this version, have the team members choose cards that represent how they see themselves as part of the team now and how they want to be in the future. There are no right or wrong answers in this exercise. It should promote in-depth discussion.

10. Fortune Teller Alternate Version #2

Description: In this version, have the team create a final card on large piece of paper with colored pens as a vision of what the group hopes the team will be in the future. You can hang this art piece where the team members can see it as a reminder.

11. **Team Slogan**

Purpose: Teambuilding

Group Size: 4+

Level: Basic

What do you need? Paper, pencils, and a list of company slogans

How much time does it take? 20+ minutes (10 minutes of prep time)

Description: Begin the discussion by talking about different companies and their slogans. Give the team some examples you have selected. Have members pick a famous slogan that they think fits the team. Have the members share their responses and why they chose a particular slogan.

12. **Team Slogan Alternate Version**

Purpose: Teambuilding

Group Size: 4+

Level: Advanced

What do you need? Paper, pencils, and a list of company slogans

How much time does it take? 20+ minutes (10 minutes of prep time)

Description: After you complete the first exercise, have the team brainstorm to create a team slogan. Begin by having them list nouns, verbs, adverbs, and adjectives that represent the team. Here is a sample list:

- Fast
- Funny
- White

- Horse
- Food
- Quickly

Now have each team member use some of the words from that list to create one sentence that captures the essence of the group. Have the team members share their slogans. Vote to see which is best. Write or print out the selection and post it for the team to see and enjoy.

Note: Some team members may be better at wordsmithing than others. That is fine; just keep things moving. In the end, everyone will vote about the final product.

13. **The Twenty-Foot Monster**

    Purpose: Trust, cooperation

    Group Size: 5+ (the larger the group the more fun the activity)

    Level: Basic

    What do you need? Strips of cloth, room to move around in

    How much time does it take? 10+ minutes

    Description: Have the team stand in a straight line. Tie each team member's legs together with the person next to him or her. Tie the two end people together. Now have them walk as a group across the room. This can be challenging for some groups. If you need to, you can break the large group into smaller groups. Make sure there are no obstacles or anything someone could fall on and get hurt.

    Discuss with the team how they felt having to work as one entity. What happened if one person would not work with the others? Was there a certain amount of trust involved with the activity? Did they feel safe with the other team members holding them up and making sure they did not fall?

14. **Can You Stand It?**

    Purpose: Trustbuilding

Group Size: 4+ (in groups of 2)

Level: Basic

What do you need? No extra materials are needed

How much time does it take? 5+ minutes

Description: Have the pairs sit back to back. Have the team members lock arms with their partners. The task is to get to a standing position without unlocking arms. The team that gets to their feet first wins.

Discuss what they had to do to communicate. How did they cooperate? How did they accomplish the task?

15. Can You Stand It? Alternate Version

Description: Once the pairs have successfully mastered getting up, have them try it as larger groups. Increase the size of the groups until the entire team can do it as one large group. This may take a few sessions.

16. Let's Put On a Show

Purpose: Getting to know your team

Group Size: 6+ (at least 2 groups)

Level: Advanced

What do you need? Materials to make puppets like socks, glue, buttons, colored felt, etc.

How much time does it take? 20+ minutes

Description: The team is broken into two groups. Each group should come up with a puppet show in which the puppets talk about how it feels to be part of a team. As a team leader, you can alter the theme, as appropriate. The groups then create the puppets and perform the shows for each other. The team should discuss the feelings and the issues that were raised. Is this an easier way to talk about issues? Does it make it harder? Were people's feelings hurt? Was there a consensus on the script for the show? How were the two shows different?

17. **The Big Tournament**

Purpose: Teamwork

Group Size: 12+ (multiple teams)

Level: Advanced

What do you need? Materials needed depend on the exercises chosen, paper and pencil for the judges

How much time does it take? 2+ hours (30+ minutes of prep time)

Description: This is a multiexercise challenge. Your team will compete with other teams for a prize. Each team must choose a team leader. These leaders then switch teams and become the team judges.

Before the tournament, the leader must choose a list of challenges. These can be chosen from other exercises in this book. The exercise is designed to create healthy competition to see if your team has been learning from the teambuilding exercises and can put what they learned into practice.

Each team has the same list of challenges and can pick any one they want. The judges decide whether or not the challenges were completed. The team with the most challenges completed wins. You can set a time limit of two hours or you can make it a day long event. Each team leader should have a discussion with their team.

Discuss what it felt like working as a team against others. Did the challenge make the teamwork better or worse? Were some team members highly competitive? Were some team leaders left out? How did it feel to win or lose the tournament? Did the team members feel a sense of pride in being a part of the team?

18. **Bridge Over Happy Waters**

Purpose: Getting to know your team

Group Size: 4+

Level: Basic

What do you need? 1-foot long rectangular pieces of paper, markers, tape (optional)

How much time does it take? 20+ minutes (10 minutes of prep time)

Description: Give the team the pile of paper and markers. Have them write down something they bring to the team such as a talent, strength, or skill. If they feel that they have more than one strength, have them fill out another "plank."

When they are finished writing down their strengths, tell them that there is a river rushing through the middle of the room (you may want to mark the river off with tape). Have the members make a bridge over the river (at least two planks wide). If there are not enough planks, have the team members create more planks by writing down more strengths that they bring to the team. Have the team cross the river via the bridge they created.

Have a discussion with the team about the creation of the planks. Could one person have enough planks to create the bridge? Was it a team effort? How did people feel about writing down their strengths and sharing them with the team? Are there any planks that other team members would add for particular members of the team?

19. **Surveys**

Purpose: Getting to know your team

Group Size: 4+

Level: Advanced

What do you need? Paper, pens, and a dry eraseboard or flipchart

How much time does it take? 20 minutes (20 minutes of prep time)

Description: The leader must make up a survey for the team to fill out. The team members must complete the survey and return it to the team leader. The leader then writes down the results on the board and uses them as a springboard for further discussion. The answers should be anonymous.

The questions in the survey should be written in metaphor form with only two possible answers. Here is an example:

A task is accomplished by the group is like a (tortoise) or (hare).

The team leader should discuss with the team how it felt to give their answers anonymously. Were they more honest? Were they surprised by the results? The team leader should use it as an opportunity to work on different issues that are currently impacting the team. Here is a list of other possible survey questions:

- The group makes a decision like a (super train) or like a (moped)

- Decisions made by the leaders are like (Sunday comics) or (a best seller book)

- Getting a raise occurs (once a year) or (once in blue moon, and there has not been a blue moon in century)

Be creative and make the theme of the questions timely.

20. Show Me Your Sign

Purpose: First impressions

Group Size: 4+

Level: Advanced

What do you need? Materials needed depend on the exercises chosen, sticky labels

How much time does it take? 20+ minutes (in addition to the activity chosen)

Description: The leader picks another activity from the communication or teambuilding section in this book. The leader creates labels and sticks them on the back of each team member without that person knowing what it says; only the other team members can see the sign. The team members should interact with other members according to their signs. When they complete the other activity that was chosen, ask each team member what they think his or her sign says. Then allow the team members to look at their own labels.

Discuss with the team members how they felt to have a particular sign. Did they feel they were treated differently? Did they treat others differently according to their sign? How do these signs affect the team in their interactions with one another?

21. Secret Admirer

Purpose: Getting to know your team

Group Size: 4+

Level: Advanced

What do you need? Pens, envelopes, and enough slips of paper for each team member to make a comment about every other team member. Here is an example for a team of four members:

3 for each person x 4 people = 12 slips of paper

How much time does it take? 20+ minutes

Description: Each person will receive an envelope with slips of paper and should write his or her name on the envelope. The envelopes should be passed to the left. Each team member should write one nice thing about the person whose envelope they have on the slip of paper. When they are finished, they are to put the slip of paper back into the envelope. The envelopes are then passed to the left and the procedure is repeated. When everyone has had a turn, the team leader will collect the envelopes. He will call a person to the front and pull the slips of paper out and read them individually. The person must guess who the secret admirer is that wrote the comment on the slip. This is repeated for each team member.

The leader should discuss how the team felt getting positive comments from other team members. How did it feel when it was revealed that you wrote the comment? Would they have preferred it remained anonymous? How did it feel to know that other team members had such high esteem for them?

22. **What Is Your Fortune?**

Purpose: Getting to know your team

Group Size: 4+

Level: Basic

What do you need? Fortune cookies

How much time does it take? 20+ minutes (60 minutes of prep time if you make the cookies)

Description: You may add your own fortunes and positive affirmations to the group in these cookies. You may also ask them questions about the future of the group. When the person opens the cookie they must answer the question. Here are some examples:

- Where do you see the team in five years?

- What was your favorite activity with the team?

- What is your hope for the team in the future?

- How would you describe the team's function to someone?

- Why are you glad to be on the team?

Keep the questions light and fun. This can be used as a celebration or final activity for a longer teambuilding session.

23. What Is Your Fortune? Alternate Version

Description: If you or the team members are good at cooking, here is a fortune cookie recipe that you may want to try:

Ingredients:

- 2 large egg whites

- 1/2 teaspoon pure vanilla extract

- 1/2 teaspoon pure almond extract

- 3 tablespoons vegetable oil

- 8 tablespoons all-purpose flour

- 1-1/2 teaspoons cornstarch

- 1/4 teaspoon salt

- 8 tablespoons granulated sugar

- 3 teaspoons water

Preparation:

1. Preheat oven to 300° F. Grease two 9 x 13 baking sheets.

2. In a bowl, lightly beat the egg whites, vanilla, almond, and vegetable oil until frothy, but not stiff.

3. Sift the flour, cornstarch, salt and sugar into a separate bowl.

4. Stir the water into the flour mixture.

5. Add the flour mixture and the egg white mixture and stir until you have a smooth batter. The batter should not be runny, but should drop easily off a wooden spoon.

6. Place tablespoons of batter onto the cookie sheet. Try to space the drops 3 inches apart. Gently tilt the baking sheet back and forth and from side to side so that each tablespoon of batter forms into a circle. Each circle should be about 4 inches in diameter.

7. Bake until the cookies turn golden brown and are easy to remove from the baking sheet with a spatula. This should take about 14 to 15 minutes.

8. You must be able to work quickly so that the cookie does not harden. Flip the cookie into your hand with spatula (you may want an oven mitt if they are too hot.) Place your fortune in the middle of a cookie. Fold the cookie in half, then gently pull the edges downward over the rim of a glass. When the cookie is completed, place it in a muffin tin to cool and retain its shape.

Discuss what the group felt about the projections of the team in the future.

24. Little House on the Table

Purpose: Teambuilding

Group Size: 4+ (if the group is too large, break into smaller groups)

Level: Advanced

What do you need? A gingerbread house kit (these can be found during most holidays), a food color pen or colored frosting tube

How much time does it take? 20+ minutes

Description: Have the team construct the house. Make sure that, as they are building, they are including each member's name in the house. The names should be placed in reference to how they fit into the team. For example, a person may have his name on the wall if he is a good support.

When the team is finished, they can display their house. They are to explain why they chose to put names in certain places. This can be displayed for the holidays at the office, or better yet, bring out napkins and let the team eat it.

25. Superheroes

Purpose: Team morale booster

Group Size: 6+ (at least 2 teams)

Level: Advanced

What do you need? Paper and pens

How much time does it take? 20+ minutes

Description: Each group is assigned to create a story in which all members of the other team are included. Each character has a superpower that correlates to a skill he or she brings to the group.

Here is a list of example:

- Supportive = super strength

- Fast worker = super speed

- Foundation of the group = can turn themselves into stone

- Can see a problem and fix it = super sight

The story they create is about the members of the other group using their superpowers to beat the bad guys. The stories are shared at the end with the other group.

The leader should explore how it felt to be a superhero. Were the superpowers chosen the same powers that the people would have chosen themselves? Was anyone surprised about his or her superpower?

26. **Superheroes Alternate Version**

Description: In this version, a comic book is created about the group. This works well with an artistic team. The team members must give the team a superhero team name. They must create names for the superheroes according to their superpower and they must create costumes for the superheroes.

27. **The Votes Are In**

Purpose: Team morale booster

Group Size: 5+

Level: Advanced

What do you need? Pen and paper

How much time does it take? 30+ minutes

Description: Each team member writes a speech about why they should be voted onto the team. This speech should include their positive traits and what they can do for the team. This should be short (about a page). When everyone is finished, they should read their speech to the team and everyone should applaud when they have finished.

How did it feel to be applauded for? How did it feel to write nice things about yourself and keep it strengths based?

28. The Votes Are In Alternate Version #1

Description: In this version, the team members create a campaign. This includes posters and buttons to vote for the candidate. There should be a festive atmosphere. You can have them create political positions that they need to be voted for (these can be real or made up). Everyone should cheer after the speech.

How did it feel to campaign for yourself? Was it competitive? Did you have loyal supporters?

29. The Votes Are In Alternate Version #2

Description: In this version, there should be two or three people that are candidates; the rest of the team are the supporters. There should be a debate about how to handle certain issues impacting the team. The team leader should proctor it. The team should vote for the person who had the best resolutions to team problems. The leader will ask how these resolutions can actually be used.

Did everyone have input into the campaign and issues being discussed? Do just the higher officials at the company make decisions without asking the employees? How does this feel? How does this impact the team?

30. Me and My Shadow

Purpose: Team morale booster

Group Size: 5+

Level: Basic

What do you need? Paper, colored pens

How much time does it take? 10+ minutes

Description: Have each team member draw his or her shadow on the piece of paper. This is basically a body outline. Now have each team member label the different parts of his or her shadow with positive attributes like:

- Head: good thinker

- Legs: good dancer

- Eyes: can see problems clearly

- Mouth: words of encouragement for others

Have the team members share their shadows with the group. Was it hard for them to think of positive aspects? Did they see themselves differently? Did they agree with what was written on other people's shadows?

31. Me and My Shadow Advanced Version

Description: In this version, everyone on the team fills in the different body parts on each other's shadows. The shadows should be labeled and passed to the left for one minute before being passed to the next person until everyone has had a chance to write on each.

How did people feel about what their team members wrote? Would they agree with other people's assessments of them? Did they learn about new strengths in themselves?

32. Personal Advertisements

Purpose: Team morale booster

Group Size: 4+

Level: Advanced

What do you need? Poster, markers, crayons, paints

How much time does it take? 20+ minutes

Description: In this exercise, the team will each be given a poster. They must create a bright and colorful poster that advertises them. It should say what their positive attributes are and contain pictures or scenes that reflect that person. The posters should be hung up as a reminder of people's strengths.

How did people feel about creating a personal advertisement? Was it hard to create something positive about themselves?

33. Personal Advertisement Alternate Version

Description: In this version, the focus of the advertisements should be about the team and the team's strengths. This can be an individual project or the team can create one together.

How did people feel about writing positive things about the team? Did everyone say the same things or did people write different strengths?

34. Newspaper Personals

Purpose: Team morale booster

Group Size: 4+

Level: Advanced

What do you need? Paper and pen

How much time does it take? 15+ minutes

Description: In a paragraph or less, a person should write a personal ad. It should describe positive attributes and strengths.

The paragraphs are written anonymously. The leader should read them aloud and allow the team to guess whose personal ads they are.

How did the team members feel about advertising themselves for a team to hire? Did they feel it was hard to sell their positive attributes? Was a paragraph too much or too limiting?

35. Newspaper Personals Alternate Version

Description: In this version, the group will create an ad about the team to try to sell the team to a company. It should include positive attributes about the team and its members and should be limited to two paragraphs.

Did everyone participate? Did everyone feel they had input in the ad? Would they hire a team with that kind of advertisement? Why or why not?

36. Awesome Begins With A

Purpose: Team morale booster

Group Size: 5+

Level: Advanced

What do you need? Paper and pen

How much time does it take? 10 minutes

Description: In this game, the team leader must pick a letter of the alphabet. The team has to come up with words that describe positive things about other team members with the appropriate letter. For example if the letter "A" is chosen then the list might look like this:

- John: Awesome
- Kate: All Star

- Sarah: Always on time

- Loreena: Appreciative

You can add as many words to people's names as you wish as long as the word or phrase begins with the letter chosen.

How did the team members feel about the words chosen for them? Did they agree with these attributes?

37. **Awesome Begins With A Alternate Version**

Description: In this version, the team is split up into smaller groups. Each group is given the list of the other group member's names. A letter is given and a time limit is enforced. The groups must try to attribute as many words as possible and make sure that everyone has been given at least one attribute. The team with the most words wins.

How did it feel for your team to compete to write good words about you?

38. **Talent Show**

Purpose: Getting to know your team

Group Size: 4+

Level: Advanced

What do you need? Materials needed depend on each person's talent. Each person is responsible for his or her own props.

How much time does it take? 60+ minutes

Description: Each team member should be given five minutes or less and should pick a talent that he or she is good at. Team members should try to choose something that the group did not know about (like blowing big bubbles or hula hooping) and everyone should applaud. No talent is too big or small.

The leader should ask if anyone was surprised by someone's talent. What was it like to get applause from your peers? How could these talents enhance the team's working relationship and how can they be applied to what the team does?

39. A Queen for A Day

Purpose: Team morale booster

Group Size: 3+

Level: Advanced

What do you need? A chair/throne, a crown, treasures such as candies or small toy items, paper, and pen

How much time does it take? 30+ minutes (some prep time may be needed if you create a crown or decorate the throne)

Description: Each person must write something nice about every member on the team. The compliments should be short and simple.

Team members take turns sitting in the throne. They put on the crown. The other team member bows says something nice about the royal person and leaves him or her a small gift. Each person should have time on the throne.

How did the team members feel about being on throne? How did they feel about bowing and bringing a team member a gift? Did this exercise make team members feel good about themselves?

40. Destruction of Property

Purpose: Team morale booster

Group Size: 4+

Level: Advanced

What do you need? Different color spray paint cans, paint masks, a large piece of butcher paper or an old white bedsheet. This activity should be done outdoors on a day that is not windy, and team members should wear old clothes.

How much time does it take? 20+ minutes (10 minutes of prep time)

Description: The team will make creative graffiti. They are to spray paint the sheet and write people's names and something positive about them. They can be creative. The sheet can be on the ground or hung on a wall. Make sure the paint will not get on any important structure. Set grounds rules for safety with the group. Make sure the painting dries before touching or moving it.

How did team members feel about seeing their names with positive traits around it? Did the activity bring the team members closer together?

41. **Destruction of Property Alternate Version**

    Description: In this version, the team is paints logos and words about the team rather than individuals. They should use words that promote positive aspects of the team.

42. **Team Banner**

    Purpose: Group identity

    Group Size: 4+

    Level: Advanced

    What do you need? Paper, pen, material to make a flag such as felt, scissors, glue, and paint pens

    How much time does it take? 30+ minutes (may need to be completed over multiple sessions)

Description: The team creates a team banner. This banner should represent the positive aspects of the group. The team should draw the banner first and color if they want to. Then the actual banner will need to be cut and decorated. When completed, the banner can be hung where all the team members can see it.

Were all the team members included in the process? Did they feel that the banner included everyone's ideas about the team? Did it help the team feel like they were a part of something important and worthwhile? How does the team feel when they see the banner hanging?

43. **Team Mall**

     Purpose: Identify individual strengths

     Group Size: 4+

     Level: Advanced

     What do you need? A piece of butcher paper for each team member, paints, brushes, water, newspaper

     How much time does it take? 45+ minutes (30 + minutes of prep and clean up time)

     Description: Each team member will create a store front in the Team Mall. The store should represent them. It should contain items that represent their positive aspects and skills. They are to paint the storefront full size. The paint should dry and then the room will be turned into the Team Mall as all of the store fronts are hung up. Each team member should explain his or her store.

     How did team members decide what their stores would be? How did team members feel when the mall was constructed? Did the mall feel drab or exciting?

44. Personal Stamps

Purpose: Getting to know your team

Group Size: 4+

Level: Advanced

What do you need? Paper, pen, colored markers

How much time does it take? 15+ minutes

Description: Team members create postage stamps that represent them. The stamps should have a picture and a word that represents who they are on the team. The team members should share their stamps with others.

How did the team members feel about reducing themselves to postage stamp size? Was this hard to do? Was it too limiting?

45. Personal Stamps Alternate Version #1

Description: In this version, the pictures are collected. They can then be scanned and sent to companies on the Internet that turn your image into a real postage stamp. These stamps can be used by the team for official mail. How does it feel to send your image and information about your team while conducting business? Is it a positive reminder?

46. Personal Stamps Alternate Version #2

Description: In this version, people draw a simple design on an eraser and carve it into a rubber stamp (PZ Kut and Staedtler Mars are the best to use). You can have everyone create his or her own stamp or you can have the group create a team stamp.

Here are the steps in creating your own rubber stamp:

Draw the design on paper and photocopy it. Shrink the size if needed.

Put the copy face down onto eraser material and, with a dab of acetone nail polish remover on a cotton ball, gently and firmly press the back of the design. This will transfer the design onto the eraser.

Carve away the white area only. The black is what you leave. Always carve away from yourself. Move and rotate the eraser as you carve. Remember, you cannot replace what you cut, so go slowly and carefully.

As you carve, use the ink pad to stamp your image. This will show you how you are progressing.

When the carving is done, use a knife to carefully trim away the excess from the design. You should leave about a quarter inch border. You can mount the carving onto a clear acrylic block using double-sided tape.

You can use the stamp on anything you use with the team or for business. It is a great reminder of the group and the group spirit.

47. **Fortune Balloons**

   Purpose: Team morale booster

   Group Size: 4+

   Level: Basic

   What do you need? Balloons, markers, slips of paper

   How much time does it take? 10+ minutes

   Description: The leader writes everyone's name on a different balloon. The balloons are passed around the team. Each person writes a small positive affirmation for the person's balloon. The balloons are passed around until everyone has put his or her fortune in the balloon. The balloons are blown up and sealed. People grab their balloons. Now the team members may break their balloons with anything but their hands and feet to get to the fortunes inside.

How did they feel about the fortunes they found inside their balloon? Was it exciting to pop their balloons and find the positive affirmations?

48. Skill Hunt

Purpose: Getting to know your team

Group Size: 4+

Level: Advanced

What do you need? Pen and paper

How much time does it take? 15+ minutes

Description: The leader will instruct each team member to write down any positive skill or trait that he or she brings to the team. When the team members have completed their lists, they must hunt down other people and their lists. They are to write down skills from other people's lists that are not contained on their own. They are given 5 minutes per 4 people. The person with the most unique skills and positive traits listed on his or her paper wins.

49. Tree of Plenty

Purpose: Team morale building

Group Size: 5+

Level: Basic

What do you need? Construction paper (brown, white, and green), pens, and glue

How much time does it take? 10+ minutes

Description: Each person should cut out a trunk of the tree. Green leaves are cut out for each team member to write on. They should glue their trunk onto the white paper. On the trunk they should write a talent that they bring to the team. They are to put their names on the leaves on one side and then the teams should send their leaves for other team members to write one talent that the person brings to the team. Each team member gathers his or her leaves and glues them onto the trunk, which creates a tree of talent. The group should share their trees.

The group should discuss if there were any duplicate leaves. Did they learn about any talents they did not know they had?

50. **Tree of Plenty Alternate Version**

Description: In this version, the leader creates a poster sized trunk. People are to repeat the previous exercise, except this time, they glue their leaves onto the large tree.

How do people feel about all the talents on the tree? Are all of these talents being utilized by the team? Are there some talents that are being ignored?

51. **Say Something Nice!**

Purpose: Team morale booster

Group Size: 4+

Level: Basic

What do you need? A watch

How much time does it take? 10+ minutes

Description: The group should get into a circle. When the leader says "go," the team members one by one must say something nice about another member in the team. They have five seconds to say the compliment. If they do not say something, they are out of the game. If someone repeats something that has already been said, they are also out of the game.

52. **Say Something Nice! Alternate Version**

Description: In this version, if three people say something nice about you, you can return to the game. Also you can change the topic and pick from the possible list below:

- Positives about the team

- Talents on the team

- Something nice about a person (the way they dress, etc.)

- Positives about the day

- Positives about teambuilding

- Progress the team has made

Discuss how some of these topics were harder than others and why?

53. **Self-Esteem Pillow Shot**

Purpose: Self-esteem booster

Group Size: 6+

Level: Basic

What do you need? Pillow case and a small softball

How much time does it take? 10+ minutes

Description: The leader holds the pillow case open on one side of the room. The team lines up on the other side and takes turns trying to get the ball into the pillow case. If they make the shot, they must say something nice or positive about themselves. If they miss the shot they must pick someone else to try and say something nice about them. If the team members make the shot, they continue to throw the ball until they miss.

How did it feel to say nice things about yourself? How did it feel to have someone else say nice things to you?

54. Self-Esteem Pillow Shot Alternate Version

Description: In this version, the foamcore board has three holes cut into it. It is propped up so bean bags can be thrown into the holes. At each hole, the person must do something different. An example is:

Hole #1. Say something nice about yourself

Hole #2. Say something nice about yourself and get a piece of candy

Hole #3. Say something nice about yourself and give a piece of candy to someone else

If the person misses, they must pass the bean bag and say something nice about the next person.

Did anyone try for the third hole? Why or why not? Did they try harder for hole #1 or hole #2? Why?

55. Show Me How You Feel

Purpose: Learning to express emotions

Group Size: 6+ (2 teams)

Level: Advanced

What do you need? Paper and pen

How much time does it take? 20+ minutes

Description: Each group is given a list of emotions and a scene they must perform. An example is happy, sad, and worried in the subway. The groups have a few minutes to work out a scene using the list of emotions and the background theme. They must include all of the elements in their play. Everyone should have a role in the scene. After a few minutes, get the groups back together and have each group present their scenes to each other. The groups must guess what emotions were used.

Was it hard for the groups to guess the emotions? Was it hard to act them out?

56. One Step Into the Future

Purpose: Getting to know your team

Group Size: 4+

Level: Advanced

What do you need? Paper, pens, and markers

How much time does it take? 10+ minutes

Description: Each person traces his or her foot onto the paper and colors or decorates the foot. The picture feet must include the person's name and one goal he or she hopes to accomplish in the next five years. The team will then share their feet with other team members.

How did it feel to share private goals with the team? Can team members help them achieve the goal?

57. One Step Into the Future Alternate Version

Description: In this version, the team creates feet to represent goals they would like the team to achieve in the next year or two. This can be done on a large poster board where everyone traces his or her feet.

Can the team accomplish these goals together? Are they similar to people's personal goals?

58. How Does That Make You Feel?

Purpose: Learning to express emotions

Group Size: 4+

Level: Advanced

What do you need? A recording of different sounds, pen, and paper

How much time does it take? 10+ minutes (20 minutes of prep time if a recording needs to be made)

Description: The leader plays various sounds and team members write down how the sound makes them feel. The team will share the results and any reasons they felt a certain way.

Was it hard to hear some of the sounds? Did they bring back memories? Did you have an emotional response?

59. How Does That Make You Feel? Alternate Version #1

Description: In this version, different songs are played. Pick songs from different genres such as country, rock, classical and gospel.

Did these songs bring up memories? Did the team members have stories surrounding these songs? Did team members feel safe talking about their feelings?

60. How Does That Make You Feel? Alternate Version #2

Description: In this version, use different pictures and scenes. Show the pictures for a few seconds and allow the team to see them clearly and get a sense about them. You can pick some powerful pictures from the Internet and magazines. Try a variety of pictures.

Did this create as strong of a response as the sounds did? Did people vary in their connection to the different pictures?

61. How Does That Make You Feel? Alternate Version #3

Description: In this version, an item is placed in a bag and the bags are numbered. Each team member must reach into the bag without looking and feel the object inside. They are to write down what emotional response they had to the object.

Did feeling an object elicit an emotional response? Did people laugh during this exercise because they were scared? Why?

62. How Does That Make You Feel? Alternate Version #4

Description: In this version, different objects that smell are placed into bags. The bags are numbered. Each team member must smell in the bag and write down an emotion that the smell evokes.

Did people have stories from childhood? Did some smells make them think about family and activities they did together?

63. How Does That Make You Feel? Alternate Version #5

Description: In this version, everyone is blindfolded. The leader takes food to each team member to taste. When one food is finished, the team members will state how the food made them feel before moving to the next food. Try different types of food, such as sweet, salty, spicy, vegetables, fruits, or bread. Make sure no one has food allergies before attempting a blind taste test.

Did people feel scared to taste a food? Did they smell the food before they tasted it? Did people have emotional responses to taste?

64. Crystal Ball

Purpose: Getting to know your team

Group Size: 4+

Level: Advanced

What do you need? Paper and pen

How much time does it take? 20+ minutes

Description: In this activity, each team member will fold his or her paper into four sections. The team members are to put their names on the paper. In each of the four sections, write one of these four headings:

1 year	2 years
5 years	20 years

Once this is completed, have everyone pass his or her paper to the right. They will write something about where they see that particular person in each of the four time frames. The paper is passed again and the procedure is repeated. Continue this until each person has his or her original paper back.

How did you feel about the predictions? Did you agree? Do people really understand you and your goals in life? Do you want to tell others whether they are right or wrong? Did this exercise make you feel good or bad?

65. **Feeling Cookies**

   Purpose: Trust building

   Group Size: 6+

   Level: Advanced

   What do you need? Large plain sugar cookies, frosting pens

   How much time does it take? 10+ minutes

   Description: In this activity, team members will decorate a cookie that represents their feelings about the team. When they reconvene, have the team members place their cookies on a plate. Team members should then pick a cookie that is not their own. The person who made the cookie will explain the cookie and the feelings behind it.

After everyone has a cookie, it's cookie munching time.

How did it feel to share your feelings (cookie) with someone? Was it hard to trust them with your cookie? Did you have a hard time explaining the cookie?

66. **Feeling Cookies Alternate Version**

Description: In this version, the team makes the cookies together. You can use heart shaped or other shaped cookie cutters to further represent a team member's feelings.

Did you enjoy making the cookies together? Were they more meaningful? Did it bring the team together?

Here is the simple sugar cookie recipe.

The ingredients needed are:

- 1 cup butter, softened

- 1 cup granulated sugar

- 1 large egg

- 1-1/2 teaspoons vanilla

- 3 cups all-purpose flour

- 1-1/4 teaspoons baking powder

In a medium bowl, beat the butter and sugar until light and fluffy with an electric mixer. To this mixture, add an egg and vanilla. Continue to mix until all is combined. Next, add flour and baking powder in intervals. Divide the dough into four equal parts. Then, shape the dough pieces into four disks. Wrap these disks with plastic wrap and refrigerate for about an hour or until firm. Preheat the oven to 375° F. Lightly grease the baking sheets. Roll out dough between two sheets of waxed paper. Cut out shapes with your cookie cutters and place on prepared baking sheets.

Bake the cookies for 7 to 8 minutes or until the edges begin to turn a golden color. Remove the cookies from the oven, let cool for one minute and then transfer to wire rack.

67. The Emotional Bus

Purpose: Learning to express emotions

Group Size: 6+ (in pairs)

Level: Advanced

What do you need? 2 chairs, paper slips

How much time does it take? 20+ minutes

Description: The leader should write down different emotions on slips of paper. The first pair comes and each person selects an emotion but does not share it with anyone. The pair has three minutes to act out a scene, each of them using the emotion they are given. The leader or another team member may pick the scenario. For example, a common scenario can be two people waiting for a bus.

When they are finished, the rest of the team can guess what the two emotions are. The next pair goes and the procedure is repeated.

Was it hard to act out an emotion? Was it hard to guess other people's emotions?

68. Emotional Dance

Purpose: Learning to express emotions

Group Size: 4+

Level: Basic

What do you need? No extra materials are needed

How much time does it take? 15+ minutes

Description: The team lines up in a row. The first person in line chooses an emotion. He or she must dance or move in some way to express the emotion. When the leader calls time, the next person must also express the emotion, but in a different way. This is repeated until everyone has had a chance. The next person then picks an emotion and the cycle beings again. The only rule is that they cannot use props or they speak during the exercise.

Was it hard to express their emotions without words? Was it difficult to come up with a new way to express an emotion you had not thought of before? Were some ways better than others to use nonverbal communication to express an emotion?

69. What's in Your Bag?

Purpose: Getting to know your team

Group Size: 4+

Level: Advanced

What do you need? Paper lunch sacks, a pile of different magazines and newspapers, glue, scissors for each team member

How much time does it take? 30+ minutes

Description: The team must do two different things. The first task is to find pictures in the magazines that reflect how the team members think others see them. These are to be glued on the outside. On the inside of the bag, they must put pictures that reflect how the individuals see themselves.

How were the two sets of pictures different? Was anyone surprised by another person's bag?

70. What's in Your Bag? Alternate Version

Description: In this version, the team members decorate the outsides of the bags. First, each team member puts his name on the bag and then cuts out the pictures of how he sees himself. He places the pictures in the bag. As people decorate their bags, they cannot look at what is inside until they are finished decorating the outside.

Was the inside and outside of the bag different? Did people see themselves in a more positive or negative light than others did?

71. **Personal Scrapbook**

Purpose: Getting to know your team

Group Size: 4+

Level: Advanced

What do you need? Paper, pens, and markers

How much time does it take? 20+ minutes

Description: Give each team member a stack of 8 to 10 pages. Give them a list of what should be on each page. They are to create pages of their personal scrap book. They can color and decorate them if they wish. When they have completed the task, they should share their book with other members of the team.

Here is a list of possible pages in the books:

- Favorite book

- Favorite movie

- Favorite food

- Where did you grow up?

- Where did you go to school?

- What was your saddest moment?

- What was your happiest moment?

- What was your most embarrassing moment?

What did people learn about their teammates? Was it hard to share personal information?

72. **Personal Scrapbook Alternate Version #1**

Description: Team members create team scrapbook pages. This version may take a few sessions, but can be fun for the more creative members on the team. These can be shared with new members joining the team for years to come. They can also bring pictures from home to add to their book.

Did team members feel closer and more in touch with team members?

73. **Personal Scrapbook Alternate Version #2**

Description: In this version, the team creates a book that represents the group. Each page contains a different team member and information about them. The book can be shared with new team members and pages can be added for them.

How did the group feel about creating the book together? Did they like having their own pages? Did they ask others to help them with their pages?

75. **What Would We Look Like as Candy?**

Purpose: Getting to know your team

Group Size: 4+

Level: Advanced

What do you need? Different candy pieces or other objects such as board game pieces to represent each team member.

How much time does it take? 20+ minutes

Description: In this activity, team members will choose a piece of candy or whatever is available to represent them. There are different scenarios that will be presented to the team. The object is for the team to arrange the pieces so that they show how close or far away the team members are during the activities. Here is a lit of suggestions:

- A crisis on the job

- The team being rewarded for a good job

- Someone is upset (the leader can pick this person)

- A team member has messed up on the job

- A team member is leading the team (the leader can pick this person)

Each member takes a turn with each scenario to arrange the pieces on a table to represent where team members are and how close they are to other particular team members. When it is a new team member's turn they may choose to leave the scene alone or they may move the pieces the way they see fit.

How were people's perceptions different? Were there patterns of particular people that are close? Are there team members that are always on the outside, not near anyone else? Why?

76. What Grade Did I Get?

Purpose: Team member evaluation

Group Size: 3+

Level: Advanced

What do you need? Pens, prepared report cards

How much time does it take? 15+ minutes

Description: The leader creates a report card. There should be ten areas that are graded. Here are some suggestions:

- Works well with others

- Is a good self-starter

- Helps others

- Does more than their fair share

- Stays late to help

- Arrives early to work

- Has a positive attitude

Each team member grades his or her own card. When they are completed, the team shares their report cards with one another.

How did people's report cards compare with others? Was there an area everyone needed improvement in?

77. What Grade Did I Get? Advanced Version

Description: In this version, the cards are given out and team members grade each other's cards. When everyone has graded the cards, the group discusses the results.

Was everyone's grade the same? Was it harder to grade another person's card?

78. Tell Me About Your Day

Purpose: Getting to know your team

Group Size: 4+ (in pairs)

Level: Advanced

What do you need? No extra materials are needed

How much time does it take? 15+ minutes

Description: The team members are paired off and one is chosen as the talker and the other as the listener.

The talker tells the other person in 8 minutes what he does in a typical day at his job. The listener must actively listen. She must only say things that encourage the person to talk more. After the time is up they switch roles.

Was it hard to talk about your job for that length of time? Was it helpful to hear other people talking about their job? Did you learn anything new? Did you feel you were being heard?

79. **What Are You Advertising?**

Purpose: Communication

Group Size: 6+

Level: Advanced

What do you need? Poster board, hole punch, yarn, markers

How much time does it take? 30+ minutes (5 minutes of prep time)

Description: The team leader will punch two holes on each poster. Each team member will get a poster and some yarn. On the poster, team members will put who they are and what they do on the team. They will take the yarn when they are finished and hang the poster around their neck.

When everyone is finished, they act as if they are at a party. They mingle and make conversation with each other. They can only talk about what is on their poster or on the poster of the person they are talking to.

Was it hard to stay focused? Was it hard not to get off topic? Did you learn about other people and their jobs?

80. **Colors of the Rainbow**

Purpose: Getting to know your team

Group Size: 4+

Level: Advanced

What do you need? Colored candies

How much time does it take? 20+ minutes

Description: Team members pick a piece of candy. Tell them to wait and reveal to them that each of these candies has a story. They must tell the story in order to eat the candy.

You can give each color a different theme. For example:

Red: most embarrassing moment

Blue: a time someone hurt your feelings at work

Orange: your proudest moment

Yellow: a time someone helped you when you were in need

Continue until everyone has eaten the candy. They may pick another piece if they wish.

What new information did you find about your team members? Was it difficult to share your type of story? Did anyone try to trade his or her candy color?

81. **Team Race**

Purpose: Communication

Group Size: 4+

Level: Basic

What do you need? A start and a finish line. These can be ropes or tape.

How much time does it take? 10 minutes

Description: Place the start and finish line about 20 feet from one another. The task is simple. The team must begin at the starting line and finish exactly together. If they do not pass the line together, they must start over. This is much harder than it seems. The leader is the judge of whether they accomplished the task.

Was this a hard task? What were the problems that arose? Was there a problem in communication?

82. **Team Race Alternate Version**

Description: In this version, the team is team is split in two. The team must still be able to cross the finish line together, but half of the team is now blindfolded. They can lightly touch other team members during the exercise.

Did the blindfolds make the task harder? How did it feel to be a burden on the team? How did it feel to have to help those who were blindfolded? How did they work it out? Was it a team effort?

83. **Times Are Changing**

Purpose: Learning to deal with change

Group Size: 6+ (partner exercise)

Level: Advanced

What do you need? Paper and pen

How much time does it take? 20+ minutes

Description: In this exercise, the team members must create timelines of their lives. They must have at least four life-changing events listed. Then the team members pair up. Each team member can choose another team member's event from their timeline. The team member must talk about this event. They must answer the following questions:

- Was it hard to change?

- What made it significant?

- What helped them through the change?

- Looking back, was the change for good?

Each team member will have a turn with his or her partner's timeline. Was it difficult to talk about change? Was it difficult to share personal information? Did the teammates feel empathy from their partner?

84. Times Are Changing Alternate Version

Description: In this exercise, the team members must limit their timelines to work. They must talk about changes they have had to deal with since becoming a part of the team.

Was this harder to talk about? Did people feel funny about revealing how they dealt with work-related changes? Were people's answers or timelines similar? Was the way they dealt with the changes similar?

85. Team War

Purpose: Learning to deal with change

Group Size: 6+ (2 teams)

Level: Advanced

What do you need? No extra materials are needed

How much time does it take? 20+ minutes

Description: The team is split up into two groups. The leader will take two team members that the team chooses. He will give them an object that they must allow a group to guess. Now, the team members go to the opposite group. They can only answer yes or no questions. The team that guesses the object first wins the round. Then yell "bingo." Both team members that played must go to the winning team. The next round begins and the teams pick a new member to play. The game is won when they have all of the team members.

Was this hard to play? Did it take a different kind of strategy? Why were certain people chosen first to play? How did the teams decide who was going to play?

86. The Cogs

Purpose: Learning to deal with change

Group Size: 6+

Level: Advanced

What do you need? No extra materials are needed

How much time does it take? 20+ minutes

Description: The team must create a clock out of the members. Each team member is a part of the clock. When the team is ready to demonstrate the clock, they let the leader know. As it is working, the leader will tap on a team member and tell them they are no longer part of the clock. The team must work out a new plan for their clock. This is done a few times.

How did it feel to have to redesign the clock? How did it feel to be removed from the team? Was every part important?

87. The Cogs Alternate Version

Description: The team is split in half during this version. One group is asked to create the clock with their members. Once they have it working, a new member is added from the other group. This continues until all of the team members are working as a part of the clock.

Was it hard to have new members join the clock? Did every person fit well?

88. Make a New Team

Purpose: Create a team identity

Group Size: 4+ members

Level: Advanced

What do you need? A picture of the team (one for each team member), paper, scissors, glue

How much time does it take? 15+ minutes

Description: Each team member is given a picture of the team. They must cut it up into tiny pieces and create a new picture using the pieces. The team should share their creations with each other.

Was it hard to create something new? Was the new picture better than the original?

89. Make a New Team Alternate Version

Description: In this version, the collage is supposed to represent what they hope the team will look like in a few years. Each team member must share and explain his or her creation.

Was this harder to do? What was different between the two pictures? Were team members' pictures similar?

90. Pinky's Up

Purpose: Learning to deal with change

Group Size: 4+ (at least 2 groups)

Level: Advanced

What do you need? 10 to 15 piece children's puzzles, a watch

How much time does it take? 20+ minutes

Description: The groups are each given a puzzle. In this exercise, the teams are asked to complete their puzzles. Once they have done this, have them do it again, and ask them to improve their time. Now tell them on the third run, that no one can use their pinky fingers. If anyone's pinky finger touches a puzzle piece, the group must start over. Whatever team finishes first wins.

Was it hard to complete the same task when there was a change? Were some team members able to change easier than others?

91. Pinky's Up Alternate Version #1

Description: In this version, tell the team that they cannot use another finger to complete the puzzle. Keep removing fingers until they are down to a thumb. Whatever team has the best combined times wins.

92. Pinky's Up Alternate Version #2

Description: In this version, once all of the fingers are removed, have each team member only use one hand to complete the puzzle. If they can complete this, have the team members only use their thumbs to complete the puzzle. This will take real teamwork to complete.

Was it hard to rely on others to complete the challenge? Did people give up?

93. What Is It?

Purpose: Teamwork

Group Size: 4+

Level: Advanced

What do you need? Pen, paper, 5 similar objects (like a tennis ball, softball, baseball, etc.)

How much time does it take? 10+ minutes

Description: Have the team members pick an item from the five. They must draw a picture of the item with their nondominant hand. When they are finished, have each member show his or her picture. The team will vote on which object they think it is. The one with the most right guesses wins.

How did it feel to do a simple task differently? Was it frustrating? How did it feel when people did not recognize what you drew?

94. **What Is It? Alternate Version #1**

   Purpose: Teamwork

   Group Size: 4+

   Level: Advanced

   What do you need? Pen, paper, 5 similar objects

   How much time does it take? 10+ minutes

   Description: In this version, the team members must use their toes to draw the object. The team member that has the most team members correctly guess their drawing wins.

   How did it feel to just barely accomplish this simple task? Did anyone give up? Was it frustrating to know you could do it easier the way you wanted to do it (with your dominant hand)?

95. **What Is It? Alternate Version #2**

   Description: In this version, the team members can use any hand they wish. This time they must draw the object from memory and keep their eyes closed.

Were you surprised how far off you were in drawing your object? Can your senses fool you?

96. **You Drive, I'll Shift**

Purpose: Teamwork

Group Size: 4+ (in pairs)

Level: Basic

What do you need? Pen and paper

How much time does it take? 10+ minutes

Description: The team leader picks a simple shape to draw like a line or circle. One partner holds the pen steady on the paper. They cannot move the pen. The other team member must move the paper underneath the pen to draw the shape. The one that comes the closest to drawing the shape wins. You can alternate partners.

Were simple shapes hard to draw? Was it frustrating to stand still while someone else completed the job? Did you try to tell them what to do? Did they get angry?

97. **Group Mirror**

Purpose: Communication

Group Size: 6+

Level: Advanced

What do you need? No extra materials are needed

How much time does it take? 10+ minutes

Description: The team gets into a circle and the team leader randomly assigns each member a number. The team will then say their numbers in order. The team must pay attention to this order because they must stare at the person whose number is after them.

1 looks at 2, 2 looks at 3, and so on. The last number looks at the first number.

The team leader should make sure that everyone knows the person they are looking at. If the person you look at moves, you must make the same exact move. It can be anything from an itch to a cough. The task is for the team to freeze in position for five minutes.

When someone moved, did the person watching them blame them for not freezing? Did one person's action affect the entire group? Did the group see how easy it was to blame others for their actions?

98. Flip a Coin, Get a Prize

Purpose: Learning to let go of control

Group Size: 6+

Level: Basic

What do you need? Dollar store prizes (at least one prize for each person), wrapping paper or paper bags, 2 quarters

How much time does it take? 20+ minutes (10+ minutes to either wrap the prizes or put them in bags)

Description: The leader must either wrap or place the prizes in bags so that the team members cannot see them. The leader puts the prizes in the middle of the floor.

Each team member must flip the two coins. Flipping two heads wins a prize of their choice. They can pick any prize not already chosen and take a moment to unwrap the prize. The person passes the coins to the next person. They then flip the coins. If they get two heads, they get a prize. If they do not, they pass the coins to the next person. This continues until all of the prizes are won.

In the next part of the exercise, the coins are passed around again. This time, there is a five-minute time limit. If a person flips two heads, they can pick a prize from anyone else's pile. Some people may end up with more than one prize, and others with none.

How did it feel not to have control over your prizes? How did it feel to not win anything? Was it unfair? How did it feel to take prizes from someone else?

99. That's Just Not Fair

Purpose: Learning balance

Group Size: 6+

Level: Advanced

What do you need? Tape, balloon, and a stick

How much time does it take? 15+ minutes (10 minutes of prep time)

Description: Divide the group into two groups, by tallest and shortest. Tape about 30 balloons high on the wall. Give a time limit of 20 seconds. The team that can grab the most balloons in the 30 seconds wins.

How did it feel when things were not stacked in your favor? Was this unfair? Did you feel the same way when things were stacked in your favor?

100. Doll Anger

Purpose: Learning to express emotions

Group Size: 6+

Level: Advanced

What do you need? Permanent markers and a cheap or old baby doll. It must be a doll that you can write on. Try to choose one with plain clothes.

How much time does it take? 20+ minutes

Description: The team takes turns with the doll. They use the marker to pinpoint somewhere anger manifests. For example, someone would write on the doll's mouth that the person is saying angry words. When everyone has written on the doll, the team should discuss it.

Was this hard to do? Was the doll covered head to toe? Were people creative in what they wrote? Did this help identify anger?

101. Take a Breath

Purpose: Relaxation

Group Size: 3+

Level: Basic

What do you need? No extra materials are needed

How much time does it take? 10 + minutes

Description: Have the team members sit in a comfortable way. The leader will talk the group through the breathing exercise.

1. Inhale through your nose. Do this slowly over the count of five. One…two…three…four…five. An inhalation should be inflating your lungs. Filling them with life-giving oxygen. You have a muscle at the bottom of lungs called the diaphragm. When you inhale, this muscle pulls down. This action draws air inside the lungs. Your lungs expand like balloons. They push everything, including your lungs and organs aside. So when you take a deep breath hold your hand lightly over your stomach, just below the ribcage. As your lungs inhale, you should feel them push against your hand. When you reach the

count of five your lungs should be as inflated as is comfortably possible.

2. Now exhale through your mouth. Do this over the count of five. One…two…three…four…five. When you exhale, toxic gases are expelled from your body. Make sure all of it is gone. When you exhale, your diaphragm is pushing upward, literally pushing the air out of you. Your lungs deflate. All of your organs and ribs return to their normal state. All of the bad feelings and thoughts have gone.

3. Repeat the process. Breathe in through your nose. One… two…. three… four… five.

4. Breathe out from your mouth. One…two… three …four …five.

5. Repeat one more breath in, then out.

Did you feel more relaxed after the exercise? Can this help as a daily exercise? Can it help focus our thoughts and emotions?

102. **Take a Breath Alternate Version #1**

Description: This breathing exercise is slightly more advanced. It should not be attempted with the team until they have mastered the previous breathing exercise.

1. Sit in a comfortable quiet place. Make sure you will not be disturbed. Inhale through your nose. Do this slowly over the count of five. One…two…three…four…five. Breath should be inflating your lungs.

2. This time hold your breath in for the count of three. One… two…three. You are allowing the body longer to absorb the oxygen you have just breathed in. It also is signaling the mind to relax the muscles.

3. Now exhale through your mouth. Do this over the count of

five. One…two…three…four…five. When you exhale, toxic thoughts and emotions are expelled from your body. Make sure all of it is gone.

4. This time hold your breath out for a count of three. One…two…three.

5. Inhale through your nose. One…two…three…four…five.

6. Hold for three. One ….two…three.

7. Exhale for five. One…two…three…four…five.

8. Repeat one more controlled breath. Inhale. Hold. Exhale. Hold.

9. Return to normal breathing.

102. **Take a Breath Alternate Version #2**

Description: This exercise is the next incarnation of the breathing exercise. Each advanced version builds upon the prior exercise.

1. This time you will use your finger to pinch one nostril close. Start with your right nostril. Use your thumb and gently push it close. Inhale through your left nostril. One…two…three…four…five.

2. Hold your breath for three. One…two…three.

3. Exhale through your mouth. One…two…three…four…five.

4. Hold your breath. One…two…three.

5. Take your thumb and pinch your left nostril now. Inhale through your right nostril. One…two…three…four…five.

6. Hold for three. One…two…three.

7. Exhale through your mouth. One…two…three…four…five.

8. Hold for three. One…two…three.

9. Now cover your right nostril again and repeat the exercise from steps 1 to 8 two more times.

10. Return to normal breathing.

Does this exercise help you become more in control of your feelings and emotions? Does you to focus?

103. **The Black Board**

Purpose: Focus

Group Size: 3+

Level: Advanced

What do you need? No extra materials are needed

How much time does it take? 10+ minutes

Description: Team members sit in a comfortable way. The team leader leads the exercise.

1. Find a comfortable chair or place that is quiet and you will not be disturbed.

2. Breathe as you have learned. Breathe in through your nose, one…two…three…four…five. Hold for three. Exhale through your mouth, one…two…three…four…five. Hold for three.

3. Do this breathing two more times.

4. Close your eyes. Now imagine you are sitting alone in a classroom. You are completely alone. You are sitting in a comfortable chair. Before you is the largest black chalkboard you have ever seen. It is clean and blank. On the desk are two items, a piece of chalk and an eraser.

5. Spend a few moments and look at the blackboard. It is blank. There is nothing there. It is just blank. Dark. Nothingness.

6. You will begin to notice thoughts creeping into your mind. They can be anything. "Boy I'm hungry." "I wonder what Jane is doing." "I am so glad I bought this book." The thoughts can be anything. As these thoughts come to mind, begin to write them on the board before you. One after the other, write down these thoughts. Fill the board with your "mind speak." Do not judge the thoughts, just write them down. Fill the entire board until no more thoughts will fit.

7. Take your eraser and begin to erase all of these thoughts. If a thought creeps back into your mind, you have to write it on the board and then erase it again. Keep erasing until you are back to the blackboard.

8. The board is black. Blank. Empty. Nothing. Blank.

9. Hold this blackboard as long as you can with nothing else in your mind.

10. When you are ready, open your eyes.

How did the exercise make you feel? Are you more focused? Did it help relax you? Can this exercise help when things are busy and stressful?

104. Sweep It Away

Purpose: Team morale booster

Group Size: 3+

Level: Advanced

What do you need? No extra materials are needed

How much time does it take? 10+ minutes

Description: Have the team members sit in a comfortable place in the room.

1. Close your eyes. Remember to be alert and try not to fall asleep.

2. Clear your mind. Now in your mind picture the worst moment you have experienced while working on the team. This is a time when teamwork was lacking. The important thing is that it needs to be clear in your mind. You have to see it, hear it, and smell it. See the faces of the people on your team and get a good picture of their expressions. Make this entire scene fill your mind and make sure it is vivid and clear. You should feel anxious and uncomfortable. Capture how you felt when this incident occurred. When the image is sharp and clear, you should feel that anxiety. Once you have achieved this, take a color picture of it in your mind. Label this picture your "worst team moment." Make sure you give it this label as it will make it easier to recall it later. Now set aside this picture in your mind. Take a few deep breaths and move to the next step.

3. Clear your mind again. This time imagine you dealt with a difficult situation successfully. You felt confident and the team was working together successfully in the face of a challenge. Like the previous step, make it clear and sharp in your mind. Hear it, smell it, see it, and feel it. See the faces around you smiling. Hear their praises of one another. Feel them tapping you on the back and shaking your hand. Feel that sense of self-worth and confidence welling up inside you. Once you feel this elation, take a color snapshot in your mind. Label this one "the moment of team success." Let the scene start to fade slowly. The colors are running out of the picture and it turns to black and white. The picture will now begin to shrink, smaller and smaller to about the size of a postage stamp. Lay this tiny "moment of team success" aside.

4. Take a moment. Pick up that "worst team moment." You

might even call it aloud to bring it forth in your mind.

5. Make it clear in your mind again. Make it clear and vivid enough to make you feel that uncomfortable anxiety. This time in the bottom left corner is that "moment of team success." It should look like the picture on a television where the screen is the large picture of a show, while in the corner is a small picture of another show playing on a different channel.

6. Once you have the image of the two pictures say: "Sweep." As you do this, the pictures change. The "moment of team success" picture trades places with the "worst team moment" picture. The "worst team moment" is now that tiny postage stamp. Enjoy and feel the elation of the "moment of team success" for a time.

7. Say "sweep" again and switch the "moment of team success" with the "worst team moment." The "moment of team success" becomes small again but stays in the picture. Feel the anxiety of the "worst team moment." Say "sweep." Now, quickly switch back to the "moment of team success" again.

8. Repeat step 7 five more times.

9. Now let your mind drift to a neutral place. It could be a park, a room, a beach, or anywhere you are comfortable and at ease. It is important that you do not skip this step. Enjoy your neutral spot for a few moments and then open your eyes. You are done.

How did this feel? Would it be worth trying this by yourself daily? Can it help the team feel more confident and overcome failures?

105. Every Which Way

Purpose: Learning to express emotion

Group Size: 4+

Level: Advanced

What do you need? Paper and pens

How much time does it take? 15+ minutes (10 minutes of prep time)

Description: The leader must come up with at least five scenarios to read to the team. These scenes should elicit emotional responses. They can be real incidents that have occurred in the team.

Each team member must make three rows on their paper: Best, Bad, and Worst

The team member must think of the best way, a bad way, and the worst way a person could respond to the situation. When the leader is done, the team should share their responses.

Were there similar responses in the different areas? Did people admit to using the bad or worst responses in similar situations?

106. **Singing the Blues**

Purpose: Learning to express emotions

Group Size: 4+

Level: Advanced

What do you need? Music from different genres

How much time does it take? 30+ minutes

Description: The leader should choose ten songs that have a message that is negative or a sad story associated with it. You should choose from different genres.

Play the music for the group. Have them write down their feelings about the songs and how they made them feel.

Did it change people's moods? Can messages change people's moods during the day? Can hearing negativity a lot affect how a person is feeling?

107. Singing the Blues Alternate Version

Description: In this version, the leader finds the lyrics of the songs. After the team listens to the songs and responds to how they feel, read the lyrics. Ask them if the words changed their mind about how they felt.

Was it the music or the words that altered your feelings? Were you surprised by the actual lyrics or story? Does music that is playing in the workplace alter people's moods? Does what people are talking about affect others who are not in the conversation?

108. Fitness Test

Purpose: Teamwork

Group Size: 6+ (2 teams)

Level: Advanced

What do you need? Balls of various sizes, hula hoop, jump rope, any other item that can be used in a physical challenge

How much time does it take? 60+ minutes (20+ minutes of prep time)

Description: This exercise is best performed outdoors. The goal is for one team to reach 50 points first. You can assign various points to complete different tasks using the items available. You might have some team members be referees. That way a few different activities can be going on at the same time. Each team will be provided with a list of possible physical challenges. The points are not assigned for just the completion of the exercise, rather for the level of enthusiasm and cheering for the person completing the challenge. Do not let the group know this until they have begun some of the exercises.

How did it feel to be awarded points for your cheering section? Did the feeling of the challenges change when the teams were awarded points for cheering? Did it make completing the challenges more fun?

109. **What Are You Doing This Week?**

Purpose: Creative time management

Group Size: 4+

Level: Advanced

What do you need? 3 blank weekly schedules for each team member

How much time does it take? 30+ minutes

Description: Hand out the three blank schedules to each team member. In the first one, they will fill in a typical week at work.

When everyone is finished, the second week is a week they have complete control over. This is a vacation week in which they are doing things they want to do. This can be anything. There are no monetary or time constraints.

Talk about these two lists with the group. How are these weeks similar and how are they the different?

The third week is a combination of these two weeks. In the middle of things they have to do, insert things that they want to do. These should be reasonable activities. Challenge the team to use this new schedule in the upcoming week.

Was it hard to create the third week? Are you more likely to do things that actually worked in your schedule than to just talk about them?

110. **Who Wants a Job?**

Purpose: Understanding leadership traits

Group Size: 6+

Level: Basic

What do you need? Blank employment forms

How much time does it take? 20+ minutes

Description: Each team member must fill out an application. The task is to pick a great leader in history and pretend that the leader is the one filling out the application. The important areas are strengths and past experiences.

Each team member states strengths and experiences that his or her person has. The first person to figure out who the leader is wins a point. This continues through the group. The person with the most points wins.

What characteristics were common between the various people that were great leaders? What defined them as great?

111. **Who Wants a Job? Alternate Version**

Description: In this version, the team members fill out their own applications. Their names and other obvious identifying information are not included. The applications are handed around the group. The team members guess who they are. The leader reads them out loud and the person whose application it is raises his or her hand. The team member with the most correct guesses wins.

Was it hard to recognize other people by their strengths? Was it hard to fill out your own application knowing other team members would read it?

112. Build a Car

Purpose: Creating team identity

Group Size: 4+

Level: Basic

What do you need? A dry eraseboard or a flipchart

How much time does it take? 10+ minutes

Description: The leader will draw the outline of a car on the chart. The team members must add parts of the car. The car part must relate to the team. An example is a window, so team members can communicate clearly.

Was it hard to build a car based on parts of the team? Did everyone participate? Was the car large or small? Was the car fast or slow? Did the car need work or was it missing anything?

113. Tap Me Next

Purpose: Team morale booster

Group Size: 6+

Level: Advanced

What do you need? No extra materials are needed

How much time does it take? 20+ minutes (10 + minutes of prep time)

Description: The leader creates a list of positive affirmations that team members can identify with. Here is a sample list:

- A person who makes me smile

- A person who makes me laugh

- A person I trust

- A person I admire

- A person who is a hard worker

The leader asks one person to stand up. The rest of the team lays down their heads. The leader reads one of the affirmations. The person standing picks a person who fits this description. The chosen person stands and joins the first person. The leader reads another one and those standing pick one person each who fits that description until everyone is eventually standing. A new person is chosen to start and the game can be repeated using new affirmations.

How did it feel to be chosen for a particular affirmation? Did you have any difficulty finding someone who fit a particular affirmation?

114. The Judges Say?

Purpose: Identifying your team role

Group Size: 6+

Level: Advanced

What do you need? No extra materials are needed

How much time does it take? 20+ minutes

Description: Each team member is asked to think of four reasons that the team needs them. Each team member must yell, scream, dance or do whatever it takes to convince the team that they should be a member. They will be judged by the team leader and other team members. Humor, loudness, and originality are all factors. The team should give them a rating from 1 to 10. The team member with the most points wins.

How did it feel to convince the team about your role as a team member? Was it hard to come up with good reasons? What did you think of other people's reasons?

115. Team Obituary

Purpose: Creating team identity

Group Size: 6+

Level: Advanced

What do you need? Paper and pen

How much time does it take? 20+ minutes

Description: The team must write an obituary for the team. It should include all of the team members and their accomplishments. It should include all of the great things the team did and why the team will be missed.

Were their items included that the team has not done yet? Were only team strengths mentioned or were team struggles mentioned as well?

116. Paper Talk

Purpose: Communication

Group Size: 3+

Level: Basic

What do you need? A piece of paper for each team member

How much time does it take? 10+ minutes

Description: The team leader will give the following instructions to the team. Do not answer questions that the group may have during the exercise. As they do the exercise, the leader does the exercise with them.

Pick up the paper and hold it in front of you. Close your eyes. Now fold your sheet of paper in half. Tear off the upper right-hand corner. Fold the paper in half again. This time, tear off the upper left-hand corner. You will now fold the paper in half again. Then tear off the lower right-hand corner of the sheet. Open your eyes.

No one will have the same paper. The leader should discuss the importance of two-way communication.

Was it fair not to be able to ask questions? Was it hard to rely on only verbal instructions? Would a demonstration of the activity help?

117. **Money Auction**

Purpose: Learning to express emotions

Group Size: 4+

Level: Advanced

What do you need? A $5 bill

How much time does it take? 15+ minutes

Description: This is an auction for the $5. Start the bidding at $1. The leader should get the group worked up over the auction and make it exciting. In the end, the bidding will go beyond $5 (you can give the money if you wish, although the leader is the winner).

Why did people bid more money than $5? Did emotions cloud people's reason? Is this technique used in the market place? Do people get worked up over things that are really smaller than they make them out to be?

118. **Verbal Wrestling**

Purpose: Persuasion

Group Size: 6+

Level: Advanced

What do you need? Tape

How much time does it take? 20+ minutes

Description: The leader makes a circle in the floor with the tape for two people to stand in and picks two team members to start in the circle. No one else may give suggestions outside the circle. The other rule is that there can be no physical contact. The task is to get the other person to step outside the circle. They can use anything in their disposal to accomplish the task. Different people can get into the ring and try it.

What tactics did people use? What were successful tactics and what were not? Were some people more persuasive than others?

6 We Have Learned, Now How Do We Use What We Have Learned?

Ask your employees what they would like to see done and how they think they can improve the workplace. Keep an avenue of feedback open at all times so that you know you are heading in the right direction. Have a general idea of what the outcomes should be and clearly communicate these points to the participants prior to starting an activity. Also consider time constraints on your employees; can you achieve the same results in less time? We all work in a world of limited time and resources. If you develop a program that eats up company resources or is a time burden, no one will support the program and probably will not participate with an open mind. In the beginning of any new programs, think small first. Maybe only offer it to a small section of the company and keep it simple. You can always add more details as you move forward, but if you start with a complex process it will be hard for you to deliver and hard for others to understand the outcome. Keep it simple, make it fun, and provide a place for feedback.

Michelle Lovejoy

Follow up is the most important step in any teambuilding exercise. We must follow up and measure the impact of a teambuilding to understand its effectiveness. Some examples:

- Solving a problem: How we can actively involve everyone to solve the problem by letting them define what they can and cannot do (have controls so that necessary steps are not missed), making them part of the solution and system

- Set goals that are agreed on by the team for a defined period of time and see if the goals are being met or not

- Root cause analysis: Once you set the goals, do a root cause to determine the success and failure, which results in lessons learned, and implement them for the next round (making it an iterative process)

I always recommend teambuilding as part of the culture of an organization. It is a continuous process rather than an event. Teambuilding exercises are critical to launch a new product, formation of a new team for an initiative, problem solving, and new hires, reenergizing an existing team…

Pramod Goel

I would recommend that teambuilding activities be done every time that new employees enter an organization. I also recommend that team leaders mix it up and keep the material fresh and interesting. The fact that an organization has regular teambuilding activities sends the message to employees that a company really cares about them and how they work together."

Dan Comer

Today's Teamwork Challenges

In the late 1920s and early 1930s, there was a lot of turbulence in the business world. World War I introduced a global thinking that had never been a part of managing a business before. Managers were accustomed to thinking in terms of providing products and services for Americans and of competing with other American companies. This resulted in the opening of new markets, new horizons, and new ways of conducting business. In addition, it was a time when businesses and managers began to aspire to bigger and better things for themselves and their companies. Surviving in that turbulent atmosphere brought entirely new challenges.

At the same time, the work force was shifting. Family farms that had conducted their affairs in much the same way for many generations suddenly found that their offspring had other futures in mind for themselves. The economic crash of 1929 forced Americans to confront their own mortality as a country and as a people. Many people did die either at their own hands or as the result of extreme privation. Populations began to explode in cities and jobs could not keep up with demands.

Living during that time put a mark on Americans that they carried with them until they died. However, compared to the business climate of the 21st century, those times seem only mildly disturbing. The glimpse of globalization resulting from World War I became a much stronger possibility following World War II. The meteoric rise of communications and technology beginning toward the end of the 20th century and at a sizzling zenith in the early years of the 21st have created turbulence, change, uncertainness, and fear that were not imagined in earlier generations. Major companies have gone under either as the result of poor management, management's failure to navigate the torrential seas of instability, or from outright greed. How can companies and organizations use the lessons learned not only from the survival of the country following the '20s and '30s but also from the important lessons of the quality movement that began with Dr. Codman's end result theories? Certainly, developing the most effective teams possible has never been more important.

Teambuilding activities can be done at staff meetings to change the flow of the meeting and get creative thoughts flowing. The activities work great when a new project group is formed or work has been hectic and everyone needs to refocus and have fun.

Deb Dowling

Effective teams are able to meet the challenges of the new work environment in the following ways:

- They can get out of the starting gate sooner.

- They can work out tactics for getting from A to B faster.

- They can use skills taught by the excellence experts to cut down on errors.

- They can take control of processes rather than being controlled by them.

- They can inspire each other to come to work every day ready to tackle new challenges.

- They can bring volume rates up.

- They can improve quality control while innovating with new ways of doing things and creating new products and services.

- They can focus on customers' needs and responses.

Follow up activities should not be too strictly structured but should reinforce lessons learned in the teambuilding sessions and give the management feedback on what team skills are being used well and what team skills need improvement.

Stephen Coenen

If you are interested in keeping teambuilding exercises a regular part of your routine, you need simply to schedule them on a regular basis. Don't wait for an unusual circumstance to start teambuilding exercises. Have a long planning meeting? A regular staff meeting? A production meeting? Start out with a teambuilding exercise to get people to focus on the work ahead. Make sure, however, that it is an exercise or set of exercises that they like doing and don't resent or it will all backfire on you.

Kim Stinson

In a symphony, if the strings overpower the woodwinds, an important part of the music is covered up. A conductor makes sure that each section is in harmony with the other. The sections look to the conductor for guidance, because musicians often get caught up in the notes. They are trying to read and perform difficult passages and often cannot pay attention to how they are blending in with others. They look up at the conductor who may hold his hand in such a way that indicates they are playing too loudly. The musician responds immediately, and the music goes on.

If a conductor did not perform this vital function, the music the orchestra was trying to perform would be a disaster. The louder instruments would dominate the softer ones. The symphony would turn into a marching band in which the aim is to be heard no matter what the cost. If the conductor was not respected or watched, musicians would become angry as the music fell apart and the sections felt neglected.

Sometimes things do not work out.

Deb Dowling reflects on an activity that was not so successful: A group of teens were working on a difficult challenge in which they all had to get over a plank wall. The group was getting tired and frustrated as they were failing to accomplish the task. Many of them just sat down and wanted to quit the activity. The facilitator was very patient with the group and gave them a needed break. They were able to regroup and accomplish the activity.

There was an activity I recall that ended with almost no results for several reasons. The true objective was not communicated to the facilitator (performance improvement versus media promotion) and therefore there was no pre- or post-event support of the program or its objectives. The program resulted in a worse case scenario for any event company . . . a very expensive, fun event with little measurable change.

Breon Klopp

You have heard the saying, "The best laid plans of mice and men ..." You can make all the right plans, set up time to do activities, have all the props, and a luncheon ready to be catered, but that does not guarantee success. One failure does not mean that the teambuilding concept is a failure. It is a learning experience that can actually be good for a team. Failure in an activity could expose problems within a group. It should spark conversation and analysis. It can propel a team forward. The point is that you should not let it get you down. Below are some comments from other professionals about activities that did not work out. They give examples of what happened and tips about what to do should the situation arise that a teambuilding activity is not working out.

Being unprepared will increase the probability that an activity will not work. It is worth the time to prepare rather than deciding to do teambuilding activities on the spur of the moment. Making sure there is minimum distraction is important. One of the worst experiences I had with a teambuilding activity was a "team retreat" that was scheduled at a children's game room pizza parlor. It was as bad as you can imagine. Flashing lights and screaming children does not meld well with teambuilding activities unless it involves which team can win at air hockey. No one could hear the other person and nothing was really accomplished. This may seem like an extreme example, but a little bit of planning beforehand could have made a much more successful day.

I can't think of an exact example. I do think that you set yourself up for failure if you try an activity in a large group and have never tried it as a participant or in a group with smaller numbers. Adding people adds complexity. If you can go through the exercise first as a participant, you know better how to explain the process to others. A simple thing to do when an activity is not working is to switch gears and try a different activity. The group will let you know either verbally or via body language if something is not working.

Michelle Lovejoy

Reflection on the experience by incorporating an aspect of the teambuilding experience into a work day may help reinforce the concepts learned.

Deb Dowling

Most people strive and desire to be successful in their personal and professional lives and few individuals set out to deliberately sabotage themselves. The desire for people to be successful and to utilize programs and training that will assist them in being successful is innate. It is the responsibility of the training organization and facilitator to ensure the program allows individuals the opportunity to improve toward future success.

It is critical for the success of the activity and for the success of future activities that the teambuilding activity be bridged to application in the workplace and company.

Persons and organizations that do not make the steps necessary toward application after a program will inevitably see little value in future programs.

A successful teambuilding activity requires an equal amount of time in debriefing and evaluating the activity, the outcomes, the effect on the participants, and reinforcing how the results of the activity are relative and critical to the actual industry of those participating.

Many debriefings are disassociated from the participants and do not seem to directly tie into the previous activity. PIT provides a debriefing activity that continues to engage the participants and build on the momentum of the exciting activity portion.

Each pit stop scenario performed by the teams is recorded on DVD for the purpose of immediate improvement feedback, as well as for use during the debriefing. During the debriefing, each participating team has at least one of their recorded pit stops shown in a group setting. While there are many applicable lessons to be learned, the disarming nature and comedic value of non-professionals attempting to perform athletic acts allows a perfect atmosphere for participants to speak openly about their personal experience and feelings. A well-prepared program will leverage this discourse into positive outcomes and additional performance-related sessions. Great times for events are to implement, modify, reinforce, and reward systems that are being utilized to meet the mission of the organization.

Breon Klopp

Sometimes a teambuilding exercise doesn't work out and that's okay. Even if the activity turns out not to be entirely successful, the team members will have the common experience and can still learn from it. When an activity isn't successful, then the discussion afterwards becomes the potential learning moment.

Kim Stinson

Recognize that teambuilding exercises are a critical step. If it is considered as a fluff exercise, STOP. Don't proceed because you will be spending lots of time and money. Senior management must buy into doing a constructive teambuilding to solve a real problem.

Pramod Goel

An example of a successful team building activity was when a common language was created among participants. I did a few trainings with this particular social service agency. They were able to use what they learned and now are among the best teams in their field in the state of North Carolina. This was only possible because of continued sessions and reinforcing what they had learned.

An example of failure among a team was when I felt that only about 5 percent of the participants learned anything and even wanted to be there. I attribute this to the lack of support by their management team. They left complaining that nothing could truly be changed in their organization and without management buy-in I might agree.

Dan Comer

Laughter Is the BEST Medicine

A 65-year-old woman was doing the nitro crossing, which involves each member of the group swinging on a rope from one area to another, and a couple of the group members needed to get a #10 can without a handle of "nitro" (water) from one side to the other without losing any water. She wanted to swing on the rope and carry the water. Everyone joined in her laughter as she tried to balance the can of water and swing on the rope without getting wet.

Deb Dowling

There are always moments in these types of exercises where everyone starts laughing uncontrollably. Go with it. Don't try to get control of the group. Let them laugh, as laughing together is one of the best teambuilding exercises ever.

Kim Stinson

Contacts

Michelle Lovejoy

Michelle Lovejoy received a B.A. in Geology, Mathematics, and Anthropology from Appalachian State University in 1999. During her undergraduate program, she participated in a research project involving glacial marine sedimentation from the Vancouver Island area. She worked as a Project Geologist for a consulting firm in Ohio, focusing on Phase I & II Environmental Site Assessments, wetland delineation and mitigation projects, groundwater remediation, NEPA, and cultural resource inventory reviews for cellular tower sites. She obtained an MS in Environmental and Engineering Geosciences from Radford University in 2004. She is currently employed by the North Carolina Department of Environment and Natural Resources, Division of Soil and Water Conservation as a Senior Environmental Scientist. She works directly with 13 local soil and water conservation districts to assist with the implementation of cost-share programs and educational outreach. She also assists with the delivery of statewide training and conferences, grant writing, and implementing Soil and Water Conservation Commission policies. She also manages the statewide contract local soil and water conservation districts have with the Ecosystem Enhancement Program, North Carolina's wetland mitigation program for the Department of Transportation. She is a prospective 2007 fellow of the Natural Resources Leadership Institute, with a project focusing on developing a training manual and delivering a round of workshops providing tools for local districts to be actively involved in farmland preservation including conservation easement programs.

As a teenager, she participated in many summer programs and leadership training activities that utilized teambuilding activities to introduce everyone and develop friendships at the start of the event. As a senior environmental scientist, she is responsible for development of agendas for statewide, regional, and local meetings and trainings. She uses many of the teambuilding exercises mentioned in this book and often starts meetings off with a quick exercise to get everyone focused.

Kim Stinson

Kim Stinson holds an M.F.A. in Playwriting from Spalding University, an M.A. in Theatre from Miami University (Oxford, Ohio) and a B.F.A. in technical theatre from the North Carolina School of the Arts. Having been a professional stage manager, directed a few plays, and taught a few theatre courses, she is currently writing plays for fun, but not much profit.

The majority of Kim's teambuilding experience is through theatre-related activities. Theatre is a natural place for exploration and experimentation with teambuilding exercises. Everyone is gathered for a few weeks to a few months for the same goal: that of putting a piece of entertainment on the stage for the benefit of an audience. Actors use teambuilding exercises all the time in classes and in rehearsals. Improvisations are natural teambuilding exercises, as are singing or vocal exercises and movement-oriented exercises. In a non-theatrical setting, no one need be a singer or a dancer, but merely to allow themselves to say things out loud and to move around themselves and each other. Just getting up and doing something together helps team members form connections and bonds, as well as understand each other better.

Dan Comer

Dan has been a trainer in the area teambuilding for the past 23 years. His clients have been large companies, government entities, and non profit organizations. He works full time developing and facilitating team building events around North Carolina. Dan holds a BS in Psychology with a minor in business. His master's degree is through Appalachian State in the Teaching Family Model. He has done hundreds of different team building events over the years.

Pramod Goel

Pramod Goel has extensive experience building business practices in startup, growth, and turnaround phases of the company across multiple industries, such as healthcare, airlines, nuclear, oil and gas, and manufacturing. While serving in senior management capacities with leading firms, he has delivered many strategic and tactical enterprise solutions encompassing operational restructuring, business process reengineering, and enterprise application implementation.

Goel's management consulting experience includes operational assessment, enterprise business modeling, change management, program management, business analytics, mathematical/operations research modeling, departmental infrastructure building, group facilitation/JAD, channel management, and implementation methodologies, while creating superior customer relationships.

Goel has strong cross-industry experience, delivering business solutions to Fortune 500 clients including Air Products & Chemicals, Alyeska, American Airlines, Anheuser-Busch, Australian Government, British Airways, British Energy, Continental Airlines, Ford, Flextronics, Huntsman, Jabil/Varian, Kerr McGee, Occidental Chemicals, Omaha Public Power, PECO Energy, Phoenix International/John Deere, Procter & Gamble, Qwest, State Farm, and Veterans Health Administration.

Goel holds a master's degree in Industrial & Systems Engineering and a bachelor's degree in Mechanical Engineering. Mr. Goel has built both internal (within the company) and external (at customer site) teams for over 16 years under different business environments.

Breon M. Klopp

Breon is the Senior Director of Development at PIT Instruction & Training. Breon is the founder and Senior Director of a motor sports facility in Mooresville, North Carolina, (Race City, USA) providing pit crew teambuilding and lean performance training programs for groups and corporations. He is a former instructor and coach for professional motor sports pit crews in NASCAR®.

The programs provided by PIT are based on the concept that, if individuals and organizations were managed and operated using the same principles that guide highly competitive racing pit crews, organizations would be more efficient, effective, and profitable.

PIT has provided award-winning (2006 Elliott Masie Learning Consortium Innovative Leadership Award /2007 North Carolina Small Business of the Year Finalist) motor sports related teambuilding programs since 2001 and has served a large number of local, national, and international organizations, including United Airlines, Intel, ConocoPhillips, Union Pacific, PalletOne, Blue Ridge Paper Corporation, Georgia Pacific, and Textron.

PIT also provides services to teaching organizations, including the North Carolina Youth Advisory Council, the Ford/AAA Student Auto Skills competition, Jostens Yearbook conferences, and school career days, including Grier Middle School, recipient of the Time Warner National Award for a physics and math teaching unit based on NASCAR®.

PIT is primarily a professional pit crew training facility for competitive teams in NASCAR®.

John Gordon Ross

John Gordon Ross is the Music Director and Conductor (1991-present) of the Western Piedmont Symphony located in Hickory, North Carolina. John has been conducting ensembles (choir, orchestra, band) since his sophomore year in high school (1966). John believes that every rehearsal is a teambuilding activity, in which the conductor's job is to assist the musicians in presenting a collective vision of one or more pieces of music. Sometimes this occurs through non-verbal communication like conducting gestures, sometimes by stopping and offering instructions, sometimes by accepting input from the musicians as to their particular needs in a given passage, such as another run through, slowing down, and working on notes and technical issues, etc.

Deb Dowling

Deb is the Vice President of Program Services/Property/Camp Director of Girl Scout Council of the Catawba Valley Area. Deb directs Camp Ginger Cascades, Lenoir, North Carolina, which is owned and operated since 1963 by the Girl Scout Council of the Catawba Valley Area, 530 4th Street SW, Hickory, North Carolina. The Web site is **www.cvgirlscouts. org**. The 265 acre camp is located in the Brushy Mountains. It includes sleeping/program facilities of winterized cabins, lodges, and tree houses. The camp has a dining hall with an institutional kitchen, a small lake for canoeing/kayaking, a swimming pool, a natural water slide on Ginger Creek, a challenge course, and a climbing wall.

Deb has used teambuilding activities at events, conferences, meetings, camps, and trainings with Girl Scouts – ages 5 to 17, summer camp staff, Girl Scout events serving 15 to 1,200 participants, volunteers in Girl Scouting – troop leaders and parents and girl/adult committees working on specific projects. She has used initiative games, low/high challenge courses, and climbing towers. Teambuilding activities are a part of most events in Girl Scouting.

Sonya Briggs

Sonya graduated from Appalachian State University with a bachelor's degree in dance. She has spent time participating and teaching in summer programs such as Appalachian State University's summer dance program and the North Carolina School of the Arts in Winston Salem North Carolina. She has studied at Santa Monica College in California as well as Velocity Studio in Seattle Washington. She has had a studio at the Tukwila Community Center in Seattle Washington and currently owns her own dance studio, Sonya's Dance Academy, in Hickory North Carolina.

Stephen G. F. Coenen

Stephen is the Human Resources Generalist at Covidien, Inc. (formerly Tyco Healthcare) in St. Louis, Missouri. He has worked at Coiden for three years. Before that, he was a member of the Human Resources staff at Saft America, Inc. for almost four years.

Stephen holds an M.A. Industrial Organizational Psychology and Human Resources Management from Appalachian State University. He received his B.S. in Psychology at Western Carolina University.

Stephen has been involved in training and teambuilding activities for years as part of his human resource positions. He has been involved in various volunteer community organizations and is currently the President of the Greenleaf Singers, a renaissance singing group based in St. Louis.

J Donald Coleman

Don Coleman is the director of the Hickory Choral Society and is an executive for Hickory Springs Manufacturing. He has the benefit of doing teamwork activities from a corporate point of view as well as from a musical director point of view.

Index